PAUL ARCHER

CeMAP 1
REVISION GUIDE

CeMAP© 1

Revision Guide 2015/2016

Paul Archer

High House Publishing

© Archer Training Ltd 2000 - 2015

This book is copyright under the Berne Convention.

No reproduction without permission.

All rights reserved. The right of Paul Archer to be identified as the author of this work has been asserted by him in accordance with sections 77 and 78 of the copyright designs and patents act, 1988. All rights reserved.

No part of this publication may be reproduced, stored in a retrieval system, or transmitted in any form, or by any means, electronic, mechanical, photocopying, recording and or otherwise without the proper permission of the publishers.

This book may not be lent, resold, hired out or otherwise disposed of by way of trade in any form, binding or Cover other than that in which it is published, without the prior consent of the publishers.

The Revision Guide, as with all our supporting material, is complementary to the main *ifs* School of Finance Textbook and will never replace the detail contained therein. It was never written to reproduce the same text - that would serve no purpose. It does contain, however, bulleted summaries of the syllabus. These bullets are lighter in substance but retain the major points.

It is, essentially, a Revision Guide.

CeMAP® and the *ifs* logo are all registered trademarks of the *ifs* University College. Use by Paul Archer of these marks does not imply any endorsement of our training material and courses by the *ifs* University.

First published in Great Britain in 2012 by High House Publishing, High House, Priors Norton, Gloucestershire, GL2 9LS, United Kingdom.

Fifteenth Edition

Printed and bound in Great Britain by Lulu.com

Edited by Lynnette Carter

Updated and edited to reflect tax year 2015/2016 Alan Downing

Cover designed by Felicia Cornish

ISBN 978-0-9571738-3-5(Paperback)

ISBN 978-0-9571738-2-8 (eBook)

For all your sales training needs, in house requirements contact Paul at

www.archertraining.com

www.paularcher.com

paul@paularcher.com

+44 (0)1452 730276

The Financial Services Industry

The Revision Guide's Contents

1 The Financial Services Industry 9
    Introduction 9
    The Bank of England 10
    Proprietary and Mutual Organisations 11
    Credit Unions 12
    Retail and Wholesale Banking 13
    The Money Clearing Process 14
    Role of Government 15
    Residence and taxation 17
    Domicile and taxation 19
    Income liable to tax 20
    The UK income tax system 21
    Categories of Income tax 22
    Benefits in kind 23
    Steps in calculating a tax bill 24
    Other Tax Arrangements 27
    Capital Gains Tax (CGT) 28
    Inheritance tax (IHT) 31
    Value added tax (VAT) 33
    Insurance Premium tax 34
    Stamp Duty Land Tax (SDLT) 35
    Corporation Tax 37
    National Insurance Contributions 38
    Economic and Monetary Policy 39
    Inflation 40
    Government Economic Policy 41
    Welfare Benefits 42

2 Financial Products 44
    Deposits 44
    National Savings and Investments 45
    Offshore Deposits 48
    Money Market Instruments 49
    Fixed Interest Securities 50
    Government Gilts 51
    Government Borrowing 52
    Corporate Bonds 53
    Local Authority Bonds 53
    Permanent Interest Bearing Shares (PIBS) 54
    Child Trust Fund 55
    Annuities 56
    Shares 58
    Derivatives 61
    Structured Products 62
    Enterprise Investment Schemes 63
    Venture Capital Trusts (VCTs) 63
    Stock Markets 64
    Real Estate 65
    Real Estate Investment Trusts 66
    Commodities 67
    Foreign Exchange 68
    Unit trusts 69
    Non-mainstream pooled investments 70
    Investment Trusts 71
    Open ended investment companies (OEICs) 72
    New Individual Savings Accounts ISAs 73
    Help to Buy ISA 74
    Endowment Assurance 75

CeMAP 1 Revision Guide

Qualifying Policies	79
Investment Bonds	80
Life Assurance Policies	82
Whole of Life assurance policies	85
Income Protection Insurance	87
Critical Illness Cover	89
Private Medical Insurance	90
General Protection	91
Business Protection Insurance	92
General Insurance	94
Mortgages	97
Types of Mortgage	98
Mortgage Payment Vehicles	99
Mortgage Product Types	101
Releasing Equity for Elderly	108
Further Borrowing	109
Pension Products	110

3 The Financial Planning Process ... 115

Financial Life Cycle	115
Gathering information	116
Contents of a Factfind	117

4 Financial Services Legal Concepts ... 118

Personal Representatives	118
Wills	119
Intestacy	120
Intestacy Rules for England and Wales	121
Sole Traders, Partnerships and Charities	122
Contract law	124
Trusts	125
Consumer Insurance Act 2012	126
Agency Law	127
Ownership of Property	128
Insolvency and Bankruptcy	130

5 The Regulation of Financial Services ... 133

Current Regulation	133
Main Legislation	134
Regulatory Aims and Objectives	136
FCA Scope and Powers	138
FCA Principles	139
FCA Principles for Approved Persons	141
Prudential Regulation	142
Treating Customers Fairly	146
Systems and Controls	148
The Senior Manager's Regime	149
Authorising Firms	151
Adviser Status	153
Retail Distribution Review	154
Mortgage Market Review	158

6 FCA Rules for Firms ... 159

Financial Promotions	159
Advertising	160
Reporting and Record Keeping	161
Training and Competence	162

7 FCA Conduct of Business Rules ... 165

Types of Client	165
Status Disclosure with clients	166
Client Money	168
Suitability Requirements	169
Suitable Recommendation	170
Executions	171

The Financial Services Industry

	Cancellation	172
	Product Disclosure	173
	Stakeholder Products	174
	Types of Advice	175
	Regulation of Mortgage Advice	176
	ICOBS	180
8	**Consumer Credit Regulation**	**182**
	FCA Regulation of Consumer Credit	182
	Consumer Credit Sourcebook CONC	183
	Consumer Credit Acts	184
	Consumer Rights Legislation	186
9	**Complaints and Disputes**	**189**
	The Financial Ombudsman Service	190
	Ombudsman's Rules	191
	Financial Services Compensation Scheme	192
10	**Money Laundering**	**193**
11	**Data Protection**	**196**
	Data Protection Act 1998	196
	EU Data Protection Directive	198
12	**Other Legislation**	**201**
	The Pensions Act 2004	201
	The Pensions Act 2011	202
	The Lending Code	203
	Banking Conduct of Business Rules	204
	European Union Directives	205
13	**Specimen Exam**	**207**

1 The Financial Services Industry

Introduction

- The Functions of the Industry:
  - Allows money to be a medium of exchange for goods and services.
  - Money acts as a measure of wealth, is portable, acceptable by all and acts as a store of value.

Intermediation

- A **financial intermediary** is a firm, such as a bank, which takes money from those who have it in surplus and lends it to those who need it.
- Like a middleman that benefits both parties by being able to attract depositors from all over the country, pulling together smaller sums to provide large enough borrowings for people, balancing their deposits so long-term borrowing can be granted.
- **Product Sale Intermediaries** are brokers who bring customers to the banks, building societies and insurance companies.

Disintermediation

- Is the opposite and where providers deal directly with the public without the need for a middleman.
- Many products which have been commoditised over the years are sold on this basis.
- Providers use branches, the internet and telephone based channels to deal directly with the public.

The Bank of England

- The Bank of England has a number of roles within the UK economy.
    - Issuer of banknotes.
    - Banker to the Government.
    - Banker to the Banks.
    - Adviser to the Government.
    - Lender of the Last Resort – e.g. Northern Rock in 2007.
- Controlling interest rates – the responsibility for setting interest rates rests with the Monetary Policy Committee (MPC).
- The MPC has to achieve a target of inflation set by the government and it uses interest rates to meet this target.
- Foreign exchange market – manages the UK's reserves of gold and foreign currencies.
- Following the Financial Services Act 2012, the Bank of England established:
    - The Financial Policy Committee (FPC) to monitor the financial sector
    - The Prudential Regulation Authority (PRA) as a subsidiary to regulate large players in the sector

Proprietary and Mutual Organisations

- Proprietary organisations are limited companies owned by shareholders. These form the bulk of the UK financial services market. Shareholders receive dividends according to profits and control the companies.

- Mutual organisations are owned by their members and do not have shareholders. Most building societies and friendly societies remain mutual along with a few insurance companies.

- The trend in recent years has been for mutuals to convert to proprietary companies with the previous members becoming shareholders and receiving a windfall of shares. This process is known as demutualisation.

"YOU CALL *THIS* A HOSTILE TAKEOVER?"

Credit Unions

- These are not-for-profit financial co-operatives that are licensed to take deposits and grant loans.
- They are mutual societies owned and controlled by their members, who must share a common bond.
- For example, members could be linked because they live or work in a particular area, work for the same employer or follow the same occupation.
- Due to changes to the Credit Union Act 1979, which came into force on January 2012, Credit Unions can now allow membership on wider criteria. This is known as "field of membership" test
- Credit unions are run by elected volunteers and, because they are member-owned, almost all profits are distributed to members in the form of a savings dividend.
- Some credit unions pay interest rates of up to 8% to savers, but most pay 2-3%. Savers also benefit from free life insurance.
- Credit unions also grant loans to members at reasonable interest rates.
- British credit unions are regulated by the FCA and covered by the Financial Services Compensation Scheme, which also protects all banks and building societies.
- Also, credit unions are members of the Financial Ombudsman Scheme.

The Financial Services Industry

Retail and Wholesale Banking

- Retail banks focus on private and corporate customers and provide a branch network to service their needs.
- Internet banking is becoming their new branch network.
- They collect deposits and pay interest and lend this money out in the form of loans for which interest is charged.
- Wholesale banks traditionally borrow large sums from the wholesale money markets and lend these out to other financial institutions or customers.
- Specialist finance houses operate in this way as they do not have a branch network.
- Retail banks use a combination of retail and wholesale methods to obtain deposits.
- Building societies also operate on the wholesale market, but can't raise more than 50% of their liabilities this way.

"BOY, THE GOVERNMENT IS REALLY CRACKING DOWN ON STUDENT LOANS!"

The Money Clearing Process

- The purpose here is to allow money to transfer from one person to another.
- Although traditionally done via branch network using cash and cheques, nowadays cards, cash machines and the internet dominate the movement of money.

Current Accounts

- The basis of money transmission for most people
- Majority of UK population now have current accounts with banks and building societies.
- People's salaries are paid directly to their bank accounts.
- Basic Bank Accounts limit withdrawals to cash machines, direct debits and the internet. This has been particularly appropriate for people receiving state benefits or pensions who previously received payments in cash.

Clearing

- The process which ensures that banks settle up at the end of the working day.
- Cheque and Credit Clearing Company oversees the clearing of cheques and paper credits. The influence of cheques is dwindling rapidly. Cheques normally take 3 working days to clear.
- Vocalink Ltd formally BACS operates direct debits, internet payments and much of the electronic payments.
- CHAPS – Clearing House Automated Payment System operates same day transfers and is ideal for sending mortgage monies to solicitors, but charges for this service.
- In 2007, the "2-4-6" clearing system was introduced.
  - 2 days cheques start earning interest
  - 4 days cheques available to withdraw
  - 6 days cheques cannot be reclaimed due to "insufficient funds"

Role of Government

The European Union

- UK has been a member since 1973.
- The UK has not yet adopted the Euro – the European wide currency.
- European laws and directives massively influence UK legislation.
    - Regulations bind the UK.
    - Directives impose an aim and let us decide how to achieve it.

UK Regulation

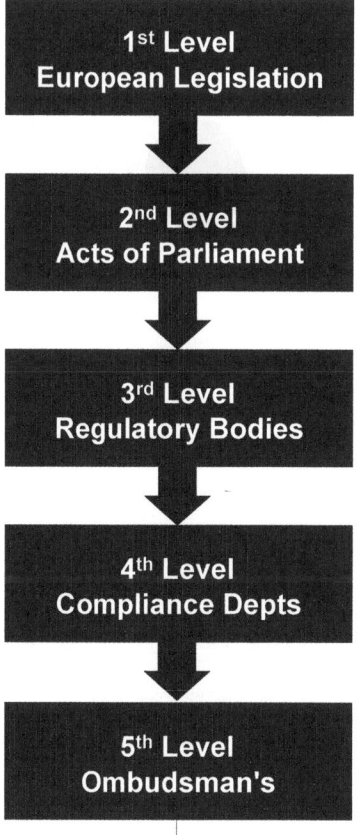

Taxation

- Governments use taxation to obtain revenue.
- The taxation treatment of investments influences investors' choices in a number of ways. Relevant factors include tax relief on:
  - Money going into investments (e.g. pension contributions).
- Tax-efficient growth and/or income, for instance:
  - Pension funds.
  - ISA's.
- Tax-free investment proceeds, for instance:
  - Tax-free cash from pension scheme.
  - Qualifying life policies.

Residence and taxation

- Income Tax is normally chargeable on all income arising in the UK, whether or not the person is resident in the UK.
- People who are defined as resident in the UK are normally liable to tax on their income, including that which arises outside the UK.

Resident

- If you spend 183 days in any tax year you are automatically UK resident for tax purposes.
- However the new UK statutory residence test ("SRT") provides a comprehensive and complex set of tests to determine residence for tax purposes.
- The legislation applies from 5 April 2013 and where an individual has previously been treated as non-resident in the UK or resident under the old rules in the UK there is a possibility that their residence status may have changed.

Overseas income

- A UK resident working abroad could be liable to income tax in that country and in the UK.
- UK income tax on the overseas earnings of a UK resident is due whether or not that income is remitted to the UK (unless he is also not ordinarily resident, in which case it is only taxed if remitted to the UK).

Double taxation agreements

- Double taxation agreements exist with most developed countries, under which normally the tax:
    - On earned income is collected in that country, but not in the UK.
    - On unearned income is waived in that country, but collected in the UK.

"WELL NOW, THAT'S A GOOD ONE. KNOW ANY MORE JOKES?"

Domicile and taxation

- Domicile affects liability to Inheritance Tax (IHT).
- If a person is domiciled (or deemed domiciled) in the UK at death, the estate on which IHT is charged includes all assets wherever they are situated. If not, IHT is charged only on assets situated in the UK.
- Domicile can be described as the country in which someone treats as their permanent home base, to which they would plan to return after every spell abroad.
- For most people, their own domicile (called domicile of origin) is determined at birth as the domicile of their father.
- It is possible to change to a different domicile (domicile of choice) by going to live in a different country with the intention of settling there permanently and severing all connections with the domicile of origin.
- Deemed domicile in the UK relates to people who, though not UK domiciled, have lived in the UK for at least 17 of the last 20 years.

Income liable to tax

- Income assessable for tax includes:
    - Salary/wages from employment.
    - Profits from a trade or profession.
    - Certain benefits in kind.
    - Certain pension/retirement benefits.
    - Gratuities.
    - Bank/building society interest.
    - Dividends.
    - Income from gilts.
    - Land/property rents.
- Some income is not assessable for tax, including:
    - The first £30,000 of redundancy payments.
    - Interest on National Savings Certificates.
    - Income from ISA's and JISA's
    - Proceeds of a qualifying life policy.
    - Gambling winnings.
    - War widows' pensions.
    - Certain social security benefits.

The UK income tax system

- The tax year or "fiscal" year in the UK runs from April 6th to April 5th of the following calendar year.
- Income Tax is based on the income received over the whole year.

Employed

- Employed persons are taxed on the amount of income in the current tax year (current year basis).
- Their tax is collected by their employer under PAYE.
- Each year they receive a P60 which details the total amount of income, tax deducted and NI contributions.
- When they leave employment, they have their P45 which gives the same year-to-date information.

Self-employed

- Income tax is on a "current year" basis, i.e., their tax is based on the profits for their business year that ended in the current tax year.
- It is payable in two instalments -- January 31st in the current tax year, and July 31st in the following tax year.
- Class 4 National Insurance is taken at the same time.
- "Self-employed" includes sole traders and partnerships.

Categories of Income tax

- Income Tax Part One
    - Employment income
    - Pensions income
    - Taxable social security benefits
- Income Tax Part Two
    - Self-employed profits
- Income Tax Part Three
    - Property income
- Income Tax Part Four
    - Savings and investment income, including interest and share dividends

Benefits in kind

- Employees earning over £8,500 p.a. (including the value of any benefits in kind) are normally taxed on the value of those benefits.
- Employers must submit a form P11D to the Inland Revenue detailing the nature and value of the benefits received in respect of these employees.
- Most directors are also included in this category even if they are under the £8,500 limit.
- Employees under the £8,500 limit are not normally taxed on benefits in kind unless they can be readily converted into cash.
- The main taxable benefits are:
  - Company cars and fuel.
  - Private health care (e.g. BUPA): taxed on the amount of the employer's contributions.
  - Living accommodation, unless it is required for the employee's duties (e.g. caretaker).
  - Interest-free loans: taxed on the amount of interest waived.
  - Child Care Vouchers above £55 weekly.

CeMAP 1 Revision Guide

Steps in calculating a tax bill

Add all your income

- Earned and unearned.
- Include gratuities, bonuses, benefits in kind, commission.
- Include all investment income and rental income.

Deductions and allowances

- Personal allowance of £10,500, income limit £100,000, where income above this slowly erodes the personal allowance.
- Ability to transfer up to £1,060 from your personal allowance to spouse or civil partner, so long as you haven't used it yourself.
- Blind person's allowance.
- If born before 5th April 1948 you may also receive an age related allowance
- Resulting figure known as taxable income.
- Deductions are payments you make on such things as Stakeholder Pensions or professional subscriptions.

Apply the Tax

- Apply the current tax rates and bands.
- Remember – some investment income may already have been taxed at basic rate.
  - First £31,785 of taxable income – 20% (base rate).
  - Between £31,786 and £150,000 – 40% (higher rate).
  - All above £150,001 – 45% (additional rate).

Tax Table 2015/2016

For use in the following *ifs* examinations from 1 May 2015 to 30 April 2016:

Level 6 Diploma in Financial Advice (Adv DipFA®)
Diploma in Mortgage Advice and Practice (DipMAP®)
Diploma for Financial Advisers (DipFA®)

This tax table provides information relating to the **2015/2016** tax year, unless otherwise stated.

Income Tax

	2014/2015 Rate	£	2015/2016 Rate	£
Starting rate	10%	0 to 2,880 (a)	0%	0 – 5,000 (a)
Basic rate	20%	0 to 31,865	20%	0 to 31,785
Higher rate	40%	31,866 to 150,000	40%	31,786 to 150,000
Additional rate	45%	150,001+	45%	150,001+

Personal Allowances

	2014/2015 £
If born after 5th April 1938	10,000(b)
If born between 6th April 1938 and 5th April 1948	10,500(c)
If born before 6th April 1938	10,660(c)
Married couples age allowance	8,165 (c)/(d)
Income limit for personal allowance	100,000

	2015/16 £
If born after 5th April 1938	10,600
If born before 6th April 1938	10,660(c)
Married couples age allowance	8,355 (c)/(d)
Income limit for personal allowance	100,000

(a) Savings income only
(b) If adjusted net income exceeds £100,000 the personal allowance will reduce by £1 for every £2 of additional income
(c) If adjusted net income exceeds £27,000 in 2014/2015 or £27,700 in 2015/16, these age-related allowances are reduced by £1 for every £2 of additional income. The personal allowance will not reduce below £10,000 (2014/15) £10,600 (2015/16) unless adjusted net income exceeds £100,000.
(d) If born before 6th April 1935 and relief restricted to 10%

Inheritance Tax

		£
Annual exemption		3,000
Small gifts exemption		250
Gross transfer	Rate	
First £325,000	Nil	
Excess	40%	
Chargeable lifetime transfer	20%	

Gifts in consideration of marriage:
from parents (per parent) — 5,000
from grandparents (per grandparent) — 2,500
from others (per person) — 1,000

Reduction on tax charge for gifts within 7 years of death	Years between gift and death	% of death rate tax payable
	0 - 3	100%
	3 - 4	80%
	4 - 5	60%
	5 - 6	40%
	6 - 7	20%

This tax table continues overleaf

The Institute of Financial Services is a division of the *ifs* University College, a registered charity, incorporated by Royal Charter.

CeMAP 1 Revision Guide

Tax table continued

	Rate	2014/2015 £	2015/2016 £
Capital Gains Tax			
Personal allowance	0%	11,000	11,100
Chargeable gains	18%	On gains falling within basic rate threshold	
	28%	On gains falling within higher / additional rate thresholds	

Stamp Duty Land Tax

The following rates will be charged on the element of the property purchase price within each tax band

Rate	Value of property
0%	0 - £125,000
2%	£125,001 - £250,000
5%	£250,001 - £925,000
10%	£925,001 - £1,500,000
12%	£1,500,001 and over

Land and Buildings Transaction Tax (Scotland)

The following rates will be charged on the element of the property purchase price within each tax band

Rate	Value of property
0%	0 - £145,000
2%	£145,001 - £250,000
5%	£250,001 - £325,000
10%	£325,001 - £750,000
12%	£750,001 and over

Pension Allowances

	Annual Allowance	Lifetime Allowance
2010/2011	£255,000	£1,800,000
2011/2012	£50,000	£1,800,000
2012/2013	£50,000	£1,500,000
2013/2014	£50,000	£1,500,000
2014/2015	£40,000	£1,250,000
2015/2016	£40,000	£1,250,000

Pension Credit
Entitled to credit necessary to guarantee a minimum:

	2014/2015	2015/2016
Single person	£148.35	£151.20 per week
Couple	£226.50	£230.85 per week

Capital (savings, but not the value of the house) over £10,000 is deemed to produce income of £1 per week for every £500 (or part) over £10,000.

Pension Credit – savings credit
Age 65 and over:

Single person	Capped at £14.82 per week
Couple	Capped at £17.43 per week

The Institute of Financial Services is a division of the ifs University College, a registered charity, incorporated by Royal Charter.

Other Tax Arrangements

Income Taxed at Source

- HMRC prefers to tax people at source to improve their cash flow.
- Examples are PAYE for employees and some pension payments.

Investment Income Taxed at Source

- Likewise, much investment income is taxed at source, but typically at the basic rate of 20%.
- Higher rate and additional rate taxpayers must pay their additional tax by completing a self-assessment tax return at the end of the tax year.
- Examples of investments where tax is deducted at source:
  - Interest from banks and building societies at 20%.
  - Interest from purchased annuities at 20%.
  - Some National Savings products at 20%.
  - Dividends from shares and equity based unit trusts at 10%.

Taxation of Life Policies

- Certain life policies such as bonds and endowment policies produce a lump sum.
- The fund pays tax sufficient to satisfy the basic rate tax liability.
- However, for non-qualifying policies, higher rate taxpayers may be liable for the extra 20% high rate tax on the proceeds.
- Additional Rate Taxpayers (above £150,000) may need to pay an additional 25%.

Capital Gains Tax (CGT)

The basics

- A taxable gain for CGT purposes arises when an item is disposed of at a price/value higher than that at which it was acquired.
- UK residents are liable to CGT on disposals of assets anywhere in the world.
- If assets are bought and sold in the course of trade (e.g. paintings by an art dealer), the gains will be treated as revenue and subject to Income Tax or Corporation Tax.
- Capital losses can be offset against capital gains.

The main exemptions

- Transfers between spouses.
- Transfers on death.
- Annual personal exemption.
  - Each UK resident is granted an annual exemption of £11,100.
  - This exemption cannot be carried forward if not used. Use it or lose it.
  - Husbands and wives can each claim the exemption against their own gains, but cannot transfer it if not used.

Exempt assets

- There is a long list of assets which do not attract CGT. They include:
  - Main private residence.
  - Ordinary private cars.
  - Goods and chattels worth less than £6,000.
  - Government Gilts.
  - National Savings Certificates.
  - Gambling winnings.
  - ISAs, JISAs, CTFs

Calculating CGT

- Firstly you need to assess the price you paid for the asset and the price you sold it for. This is the initial profit.
- Then you add any buying costs to the purchase price and deduct selling costs from the sale price.
- This will narrow the profit for CGT purposes.
- Any improvements, not maintenance, can now be added to the purchase price, again narrowing the profit.
- Gains made before 31 March 1982 are ignored. Take the value for this date instead.
- Deduct your annual allowance, currently £11,100.
- Deduct any losses from other asset sales; this gives you your taxable gain.
- Calculate the profit at 18% for basic taxpayers; 28% for higher rate taxpayers.

"LET ME START BY SAYING I WISH I HAD YOUR IMAGINATION ..."

Postponing the CGT Bill

- Roll over relief.
    - CGT is postponed on business assets where the proceeds are used to buy further business assets.
- Hold over relief.
    - Similarly, CGT can be postponed by passing certain assets on as a gift. The CGT is then payable when the person who received the gift sells up later.
    - A family business is one example.

Entrepreneurs Relief

- Entrepreneurs' Relief allows individuals and some trustees to claim relief on qualifying gains made on the disposal of any of the following:
    - all or part of a business
    - the assets of a business after it has stopped trading
    - shares in a company
- There is a maximum lifetime limit of Entrepreneurs' Relief you can claim, , which is £10 million for 2015/2016

Buy-to-let tax bill

I bought a buy-to-let property in October 2003 and was wondering what costs I can set against tax, as my tax return for the last financial year needs completing.

I know I can offset the monthly mortgage outlay but what about the actual expense of purchasing the property; for example, solicitor's fees, land registry fees, stamp duty, search fees, survey fees, mortgage arrangement fee, buildings insurance, etc?

Maggie Fleming writes: You can deduct any expenses which are not of a capital nature from the rents you receive in order to calculate your taxable profit. You need to be careful with the mortgage repayments, though; you can only deduct the interest that you pay – you get no relief for the capital element.

Broadly, the expenses you can deduct are recurring expenses – insurance premiums, ground rent, gas safety check, water rates, management charges, the cost of advertising for a tenant, expenses for granting a lease of one year or less, everyday repairs and maintenance and so on.

If the property is let furnished, you can also claim 10 per cent of net rents (usually gross rents less water rates) as a "wear and tear" allowance – this is intended to cover depreciation of furniture. If let unfurnished, you can claim for the replacement of items such as carpets.

Apart from buildings insurance, I am afraid the expenses listed by you are capital. You will get relief for these only when you come to sell the property, when they will be deducted from your capital gain. Other capital expenses you will be able to claim at that time will include improvements to the property (for example, a loft conversion or an extension) as well as the incidental costs incurred during the sale.

Inheritance tax (IHT)

- Inheritance Tax is payable on certain "transfers of value" made during a person's lifetime or on the value of the estate passing on death.
- The taxable value of a transfer is the reduction in value of the donor's estate, not the increase in value of the recipient's estate.
- If the taxable estate is less than £325,000 (the nil rate band), no IHT is payable.
  - This nil rate band can now be shared amongst married couples and civil partnerships, effectively doubling the band to £650,000.
  - Unused nil rate bands can be transferred to the surviving spouse as a percentage of the unused allowance. This ensures you benefit from future nil rate band increases.
- If it exceeds the nil rate band, the excess is taxed at:
  - 40% on death.
  - 20% on chargeable lifetime transfers..
- If death occurs within 7 years of a chargeable lifetime transfer, additional tax may be due.
- These are lifetime transfers - on a PET, no tax is due at the time of the transfer, but tax becomes due if the donor dies within 7 years of the gift.
- All is due up to 3 years, then the liability reduces by 20% each year until year 7.

IHT around the globe
- Canada, Australia, New Zealand, Cyprus, Italy, Estonia and Sweden – no IHT
- US – plans to wipe out federal IHT by 2010, though some states will still impose local taxes
- France – maximum rate of 40 per cent over a threshold of £1.5 million
- Germany – 30 per cent over a £2 million threshold.

Exemptions

- Spouse exemption
    - There is no IHT liability on transfers between spouses, during lifetime or on death.
- Small gifts exemption
    - Gifts of up to £250 p.a. per person to any number of recipients.
- Annual exemption
    - Gifts totalling £3,000 in any one year.
    - If not used, this exemption can be carried forward by one year but no further.
- Gifts in consideration of marriage
    - These are exempt up to:
        - £5,000 from parents.
        - £2,500 from grandparents.
        - £1,000 from others.
- Normal expenditure
    - Regular gifts made out of income are normally exempt provided they do not affect the donor's standard of living.
- Other exemptions include:
    - Gifts to charities and qualifying political parties.
    - Gifts for national and public purposes.
    - Certain exemptions apply to allow businesses to be passed on intact. These include business property relief and agricultural property relief.

IHT and the family home

- Currently, inheritance tax is charged at 40% on estates over the tax-free allowance of £325,000
- But from April 2017 everyone will be offered an additional "family home allowance" of £100,000, rising to £175,000 by 2020.
- It means that couples will soon be able to pass on assets worth up to £1m to their children.

Value added tax (VAT)

- VAT is an indirect tax levied on the sale of most goods and services in the UK.
- The current standard rate is 20% which came into effect on 4th January 2011.
- Certain goods and services are charged at 5% such as heating oil and child car seats.
- There is also a zero rate that applies to certain goods and services. These include:
  - Books and newspapers.
  - Children's clothes.
  - Transport and medicines.
- Supplies of certain goods and services are exempt from VAT. They include:
  - Sale of land.
  - Lending.
  - Insurance.
  - Health.
  - Education
- Businesses with a turnover of at least £82,000 per annum, are required to register for VAT, even if the goods/services they provide are currently zero-rated.
- Businesses with a turnover below the threshold may register if they wish.
- Broadly speaking, being registered adds to the administration of the business, and of course increases the cost of what it sells, but it also brings the advantage of being able to reclaim VAT paid on certain purchases made in the course of business.
- The supply of financial advice is NOT exempt, and advisers who charge a fee for their service are subject to VAT just like, for instance, solicitors and accountants.

Biscuit tax wars

It doesn't look much like a teacake (more like a chocolate-covered marshmallowly thing, in fact), but after a 30-year battle with the Revenue, M&S has established that its "teacakes" are indeed cakes – thereby ensuring a £3.4bn VAT refund. The key point, says The Guardian, is that "luxury" chocolate biscuits are liable for VAT, whereas cakes are not. But separating the two has long proved sticky. McVitie's won a battle over Jaffa cakes by arguing that "biscuits go soft when they are stale while cakes go hard". Yet when the Journal of Unlikely Science investigated the matter, it found that Jaffa cakes were actually "pseudobiscuits".

22 December 2007 THE WEEK

Insurance Premium tax

- The standard rate of Insurance Premium Tax will rise from is 6% to 9.5% with effect from November 2015.
- IPT applies to most general insurance but life insurance and most other long term insurance is exempt.

Stamp Duty Land Tax (SDLT)

Stamp Duty on Property

- Stamp duty land tax (or Land and Buildings Transaction Tax in Scotland) is a lump-sum tax that anyone buying a property or land costing more than a set amount has to pay.

- The rate you'll pay the tax at varies based on the price of the property and the type (we'll focus on residential buildings, rather than commercial).

- Sweeping changes to stamp duty were announced in December 2014. Stamp duty has been reformed - the slab system (where you'd pay a single rate on the entire property price) has been swept away, and in its place is a more progressive system.

What stamp duty rate is payable?

Purchase Price	SDLT
Up to £125,000	Zero
Over £125,000 to £250,000	2%
Over £250,000 to £925,000	5%
Over £925,001 to £1,500,000	10%
Over £1,500,000	12%

Other Stamp Duties

- The rate of stamp duty on shares is ½%, unless stamp duty is below £5

- The rate of stamp duty on bearer instruments is 1.5%

2015/2016

An SDLT example

- Let's assume you're buying a property for £300,000.
- Old system
  - You would have paid 1% on a property between £125,000 and £250,000, between £250,000 and £500,000 you'd pay 3%.
  - So because the purchase price is over £250,000, you'd have paid 3% on the entire purchase price, despite only being £50,000 above the threshold.
  - Thus, you'd have paid £9,000 in stamp duty.
- New system
  - You pay nothing below £125,000, which is £0
  - You pay 2% on between £125,000 and £250,000, which is £2,500
  - You pay 5% on the value of the property above £250,000, which is £2,500
  - So in total this means you'll pay £5,000 (£0+£2,500+£2,500).

How does it work in Scotland?

- Referred to as 'Land and Buildings Transaction Tax'.
- It's still a lump-sum tax that anyone buying a property or land costing more than a set amount has to pay.
- Remarkably similar system to the one the rest of the UK uses, the main difference is the thresholds it uses are at different rates.

Purchase Price - Scotland	SDLT
Up to £145,000	Zero
Over £145,000 to £250,000	2%
Over £250,000 to £325,000	5%
Over £325,001 to £750,000	10%
Over £750,000	12%

Corporation Tax

- Companies pay corporation tax. It is charged on the profits (including chargeable gains) arising in each accounting period.
- Self-employed, partners are charged income tax not Corporation Tax.
- Companies are charged Corporation Tax usually 9 months after their annual accounting period except larger companies who pay in instalments.
- Rates charged for all companies are currently 20%:

"YOU CALL *THIS* A HOSTILE TAKEOVER?"

National Insurance Contributions

Class 1

- Payable by employees and employers on a percentage rising scale.
- Based on their total earnings.

Class 2

- Flat rate contributions from self-employed persons.

Class 3

- Voluntary contributions which can be made by persons not paying other contributions, in order to maintain full rights to basic pension or to improve rights to state sickness benefits.

Class 3A

- Class 3A voluntary contributions will allow pensioners and those reaching State Pension age before 6 April 2016 who have entitlement to a UK State Pension, the opportunity to increase their State Pension.
- Those eligible will be able to pay Class 3A contributions from October 2015 to April 2017, when the new flat rate State Pension starts.

Class 4

- Payable by the self-employed on a percentage rising scale on their profits.

Economic and Monetary Policy

Government Aims for the Economy

- Price stability.
  - The measure is inflation which is the price of goods and services on the increase.
  - It's caused by too much money in the economy chasing too few goods. This over demand for a limited supply causes prices to go up.
- Low unemployment.
- Neutral balance of payments.
  - Imports of goods and services are balanced with equal export of goods and services.
  - Traditionally the UK has had a negative balance of payments for goods and a positive for services and the financial services industry is a great source of foreign income.
- Satisfactory economic growth.
  - The economy is growing and people's standards of living have increased.
  - It's difficult to achieve all four objectives since focussing on one can have a negative effect on another.
  - For example raising interest rates which will reduce inflation might well increase unemployment.
  - The Government has recently aimed for steady inflation and steady economic growth but the recent economic recession has caused a very slow growth in the upswing period and the economy is struggling to accelerate this above 2% per annum.

Inflation

Inflation Measures

- This is a measure of the increase in price of goods and services.
- The Government uses the Consumer Price Index (CPI) now as a target. The annual target is 2% plus or minus 1%.
- The Bank of England is responsible for maintaining this target and will increase interest rates if it is breached.
- The Retail Prices Index (RPI) is still used as an index but not strictly targeted.

Deflation

- A general decline in prices, often caused by a reduction in the supply of money or credit.
- Deflation can be caused also by a decrease in government, personal or investment spending.
- The opposite of inflation, deflation has the side effect of increased unemployment since there is a lower level of demand in the economy, which can lead to an economic depression.
- The Bank of England will attempt to stop severe deflation, along with severe inflation, in an attempt to keep the excessive drop in prices to a minimum.

Disinflation

- A slowing in the rate of price inflation.
- Disinflation is used to describe instances when the inflation rate has reduced marginally over the short term.
- Although it is used to describe periods of slowing inflation, disinflation should not be confused with deflation.

Government Economic Policy

Monetary Policy

- Monetarists believe that inflation is caused by an increase in the supply of money into the economy.
- The availability of credit is the biggest culprit to increasing money supply.
- The main weapon to control money supply is therefore interest rates.
- Alternatively credit can be restricted in other ways.
- The Bank of England Monetary Policy Committee (MPC) meets monthly to decide the Bank Base rate which influences all other interest rates.
- The popularity of fixed rate mortgages, many for long terms such as 10 years, is beginning to disarm the Bank of England because their rate changes will only affect people on variable rate or tracker mortgages.

Fiscal Policy

- Fiscal economists believe that spending by the government controls the economy.
- The bigger the government spend the more activity the economy enjoys and this increases employment and growth.
- After the war, the UK adopted this approach and nationalised many industries to create one of the biggest public sectors in the world. The Coal Board, the railways, the motor industry were all nationalised.
- These were known as the public sector.
- Then it would control the economy by spending through the public sector raising its money from taxation and borrowing.
- Raising taxation would also dampen money supply.
- Government borrowing (through Gilts and National Savings) creates the Public Sector Net Cash Requirement (PSNCR).
- Fiscal policies lost their glamour in the 1970's and for the next few decades the public sector was slowly but surely sold off to private hands to leave a small compact public sector.
- Government spending on the NHS, for example, can still generate a positive effect, but less impact.

Welfare Benefits

- Welfare benefits are an enormous expenditure by the UK government, representing about 6% of GDP, source - Office of National Statistics.
- The amount of savings is taken into account in deciding on eligibility for Income Support and some other benefits.
- Benefits are reduced when savings exceed £6,000, and is disallowed altogether if savings exceed £16,000.
- These benefits should, therefore, be borne in mind when assessing a client's need to maintain an "emergency fund".
- Welfare Reform Act 2012 introduces a new State Benefit called "Universal Credit". This is a means tested credit for people of working age.
- A summary of the latest benefits is on the next page

Self-employed get a raw deal on NI

OLDER married women have not only lost out through the married woman's contribution. Those of us who have been in business for many years – 36 in my case – have had to pay Class 4 National Insurance contributions, which do not provide us with any benefits. This seems unjust.

Jane Combes
address supplied

THE self-employed do indeed get a raw deal. They have to pay Class 2 contributions at a flat rate of £2 a week. This allows them to qualify for incapacity benefit, a retirement pension, widow's benefit and maternity allowance. But they lose out on jobseekers' allowance, statutory sick pay, statutory maternity pay and the state earnings-related pension scheme (Serps), which is an add-on to the basic pension.

They also have to pay Class 4 NICs of up to £1,806 a year for which they get absolutely nothing.

National Insurance is income tax in all but name and is full of inequities. The Government should admit as much, combine it with basic rate tax, and reform the benefit system. The notion of contributory benefits is largely irrelevant since most claimants are eligible for non-contributory benefits if they have not made enough NICs to qualify.

The Financial Services Industry

	Eligibility Criteria	Paid for	NI Dependent?	Means Tested	Taxable	Miscellaneous
Pension Benefits						
Basic State Pension	Provides a weekly retirement pension income to men above 65 and women above 60 (65 by 2020). Increasing later to 68	Until death	Yes – Class 1, 2 and 4	No	Yes	An increased state pension can be paid to those who do not retire at state pension age. Roughly 25% of average earnings
State Second Pension	Top up State pension determined by Middle Band Earnings.	Until death	Yes – Class 1	No	Yes	Paid at state retirement age. Roughly 25% of average earnings
Pensions Credit	Takes all retired people to a minimum income level set each year	Until death	Yes	Yes	No	
Family Benefits						
Statutory Maternity Pay	Weekly income for pregnant women with same employer at least 6 months. 1st 6 weeks 90% pay	39 weeks	Yes – Class 1	No	Yes	Less than 2 years with employer or self-employed may get Maternity Allowance
Maternity Allowance	Available to self-employed or mothers just recently changed jobs	39 weeks	No	Yes	No	Lower amount than Statutory Maternity Pay
State Paternity Pay	Given to biological father or partner	2 weeks	Yes	No	Yes	Need 26 weeks continuous service
Child Benefit	Paid weekly to adult responsible for child from birth to maximum age	to 16 yrs	No	Yes	No	Extends to 17 to 19 if in full time education. Removed if one partner earning in excess of £50,000
Working Tax Credit	Payable to all on low incomes	Must re-apply every 6 months	No	Yes	No	Means tested with savings of £6,000 to £16,000 considered
Income Support	To people over age 18 who are working less than 16 hours a week or unemployed	Must re-apply every 6 months	No	Yes	No	Means tested with savings of £6,000 to £16,000 considered. Those aged over 60 – now called minimum income guarantee
Child Tax Credit	Payable to families with at least one child		No	Yes	No	Additional payments for disabled children
Illness Benefits						
Statutory Sick Pay	Minimum statutory wage on sickness to employees	4th day to 28 weeks	Yes – Class I	No	Yes	Paid by employer who may claim back from DW&P
Incapacity Benefit	Benefit subject to incapacity to work 1. Short term low rate – to 28 weeks 2. Short term high rate – weeks 29 - 52 3. Long term rate – over 1 year	1. To 28 wks 2. 29 - 52 3. Over 1 yr	Yes	No	1. No 2. Yes 3. Yes	Short term high rate given to employed after Statutory Sick Pay stops. All Incapacity claimants will be moved to the new Employment and Support Allowance by 2013
Employment and Support Allowance	Helps people into work according to their disabilities 1. NI contribution-based ESA 2. income-related ESA – own or on top of contribution-based ESA	1. 13 weeks 2. – no time limit	1. Yes 2. No	1. No 2. Yes	1. Yes 2. No	After 13 weeks, paid at a lower rate to those working
Attendance Allowance	Available to those aged over 65 needing paid assistance	Indefinitely	No	No	No	Two rates applicable
Personal Independence Payment (PIP)	Given to people under 65 needing paid assistance	Indefinitely	No	No	No	Replaced Disability Living Allowance
Carer's Allowance	Given to carers of the seriously ill or disabled claiming either of the above	Indefinitely	No	No	Yes	Must be caring for more than 35 hours per week.
Job Related Benefits						
Redundancy Payment	If employee with one employer for more than 2 years	One off lump sum	No	No	No if less £30,000	Paid by employer
Job Seekers Allowance	Flat rate to job seekers	6 months	Yes – Class 1	No	Yes	Capable and available for work. If no NI record may qualify for income based JSA
Death Benefits						
Bereavement Payment	Lump sum of £2,000 to widows and widowers below age of 60	One off payment	Yes	No	No	
Widowed Parent's Allowance	Weekly payment available to widows or widowers with dependent children under 18	Until ceases dependent	Yes	No	Yes	Doesn't depend on NI record if death caused by job.
Bereavement allowance	Weekly payment payable if widow or widower aged over 45 and has no children	52 weeks	Yes	No	Yes	
Universal Credit						
	Designed to replace Income Support, Jobseekers, Employment and Support, Working Tax Credit, Child Tax Credit and Housing Benefit.					Benefit cap - £26,000 (reducing to £23,000)

2015/2016

2 Financial Products

Deposits

- Main characteristics: high liquidity, very low risk, generally variable rate of return (not guaranteed).
- They include:
  - Instant access accounts.
    - Low minimum balance, low interest rates.
  - High interest accounts.
    - Minimum balance and/or minimum notice of withdrawal.
    - Higher rates for higher balances.
  - Money Market deposits.
    - Attractive to individuals with large amounts to invest for a short term.
- Interest paid on deposits has tax deducted at 20% automatically unless R85 has been completed whereby interest is paid gross.
- Higher rate taxpayers will be liable to an additional 20%. Additional Rate Taxpayers an extra 25%.
- Offshore deposits are available from branches outside of the UK. Interest is payable gross but taxable if you are a UK resident for tax purposes.

Taxation on interest 2016

- Firstly all interest from deposit accounts, current accounts will be paid gross regardless of the account holder's position or preference.
  - The first £1,000 of interest for basic rate taxpayers will be tax free.
  - The first £500 of interest for high rate taxpayers will be tax free.
  - Nothing tax free for additional rate taxpayers.
- All tax due on the excess over these limits is payable via the self-assessment scheme.

National Savings and Investments

- The product stable for National Savings changes regularly, but saying that, the exam asks that you're aware of the basics of each product.
- On the next page you'll find the latest National Saving's guide for Financial Advisers.
- Check their website, www.nsandi.co.uk, for an updated list.

Savers fail to heed closure

BY TESSA THORNILEY

ALMOST 13m British savers still have £452m stashed away in National Savings & Investments' Ordinary Account even though it is being closed down today and customers can no longer make deposits or withdrawals.

The Government's savings arm announced plans to close the 143-year-old account last year, to replace it with a new Easy Savings Account. The Ordinary account, which could only be accessed through Post Office branches, was expensive to administer and inconvenient for customers, National Savings said.

Despite writing to all 2.6m customers who had used their account within the past two years to warn them about the changes, and extensive advertising, millions of pounds remain unclaimed.

Only one million people have so far responded and asked to transfer their funds to a new account. National Savings said about 200,000 Ordinary accounts were still being used regularly.

Ernie to splash the cash on birthday

NS&I will celebrate 50 years of Premium Bonds on 1 November, with five £1m draws planned to mark the occasion. Premium Bonds totalling £32bn are held by 23m people, almost 40 per cent of the population, making them one of Britain's most successful financial products. Pictured are Ernest Marples, the first Premium Bond paymaster general, with the now legendary draw machine Ernie in 1957 during the first draw.

CeMAP 1 Revision Guide

Quick guide for financial advisers
1 June 2015

This is not a consumer advertisement. It is intended for professional financial advisers and should not be relied upon by private investors or any other persons.

Coloured type indicates changes since last edition

	Rate	Tax	How to apply	Key benefits	Min	Max	Who for	Access
Tax-free								
Direct ISA	1.50% AER (= 2.72% gross for additional rate taxpayers, 2.50% for higher rate taxpayers, 1.87% for basic rate taxpayers).	tax free		• Tax-free	£1	£15,240 for the 2015/16 tax year	Individuals 16+ resident in UK for tax purposes.	Repayment by BACS. Min withdrawal £1.
Premium Bonds	Rate for prize fund 1.35% (variable). The odds of each £1 unit winning a prize are 26,000 to 1 each month.	tax free		• Two £1 million jackpots • Over two million prizes each month • All prizes tax-free • Prizes paid by BACS or crossed warrant	£100	£50,000	Individuals 16+. Under 16, by parents, guardians, (great) grandparents.	Funds normally received within 8 working days by BACS or crossed warrant.
Fixed Interest Savings Certificates No Issues currently on general sale	Re-investment rates for maturing investments available at **nsandi-adviser.com**	tax free SIPP		• Tax-free • Guaranteed returns • Investment options at maturity*	£100	£15,000 per person, per Issue.	Individuals 16+, (also jointly), trustees.	Funds normally received within 8 working days by BACS. No penalty for repayment at full term. Otherwise penalty equivalent to 90 days' interest on amount cashed in.
Index-linked Savings Certificates No Issues currently on general sale	Re-investment rates for maturing investments available at **nsandi-adviser.com**	tax free SIPP		• Tax-free • Inflation beating • Linked to the Retail Prices Index • Investment options at maturity**	£100	£15,000 per person, per Issue.	Individuals 16+, (also jointly), trustees.	Funds normally received within 8 working days by BACS. No penalty for repayment at full term. Otherwise penalty equivalent to 90 days' interest on amount cashed in and also lose the index-linking on whole Certificate for the year amount cashed in.
Children's Bonds Issue 35	2.50% AER guaranteed for five years.	tax free		• Tax-free – even if children become taxpayers • Guaranteed rate • No tax for parents to pay	£25	£3,000 per Issue, per child	Parents, guardians, (great) grandparents for individuals under 16.	Funds normally received within 8 working days by BACS. No penalty for repayment at full term. Otherwise penalty equivalent to 90 days' interest on amount cashed in.
Growth								
Guaranteed Growth Bonds No Issues currently on sale	Re-investment rates for maturing investments available at **nsandi-adviser.com**	Tax (at 20%) deducted at source. SIPP		• Guaranteed rates • Choice of terms • Interest taxable, paid net	£500	£1 million per person, per Issue.	Individuals 16+ or 2 jointly; trustees.	Funds normally received within 8 working days by BACS. No penalty for repayment at full term. Otherwise penalty equivalent to 90 days' interest on amount cashed in.

See overleaf for monthly income and savings accounts

Financial Products

Quick guide for financial advisers continued
1 June 2015

	Rate	Tax	How to apply	Key benefits	Min	Max	Who for	Access
Monthly income								
Guaranteed Income Bonds *No Issues currently on sale*	Re-investment rates for maturing investments available at nsandi-adviser.com	Tax (at 20%) deducted at source before income is paid. SIPP		• Guaranteed monthly income • Choice of terms • Interest taxable, paid net	£500	£1 million per person, per issue.	Individuals, or 2 jointly; trustees for not more than 2 individuals.	Funds normally received within 8 working days by BACS. No penalty for repayment at full term. Otherwise penalty equivalent to 90 days' interest on amount cashed in.
Income Bonds	1.25% gross/1.26% AER Paid monthly. Rates variable.	Taxable but paid in full without deduction of tax at source. SIPP		• Monthly income • Variable interest rate	£500	£1 million sole £2 million joint	Individuals 16+, or 2 jointly; trustees	Easy access (no notice, no penalty). Repayment by BACS. Min withdrawal £500.
Savings accounts								
Direct Saver	1.10% gross/AER Rates variable	Taxable but paid in full without deduction of tax at source.		• Attractive interest rates	£1	£2 million sole £4 million joint	Individuals, or 2 jointly	Repayment by BACS. Min withdrawal £1.
Investment Account	0.75% gross/AER Rates variable	Taxable but credited in full without deduction of tax at source.		• Managed by post only • Transaction records and annual statement	£20	£1 million sole £2 million joint	Individuals 16+ or 2 jointly; trustees. Under 16 by parents, guardians, (great) grandparents.	Easy access (no notice, no penalty). Repayment by BACS or crossed warrant.

All interest rates are pa.

Tax-free means that interest or prizes are exempt from UK Income Tax and Capital Gains Tax.

AER (Annual Equivalent Rate) illustrates what the interest rate would be if interest was paid and compounded once each year.

Gross is the taxable rate of interest without the deduction of UK Income Tax.

Net is the rate of interest payable after the deduction of UK Income Tax at the rate specified by law.

Online Phone Post

These investments may be held within a SIPP or SSAS in the form of corporate trust holding. However just because an investment is 'permitted' by HMRC does not necessarily mean that all providers will allow them in their schemes so always check with the SIPP or SSAS company concerned.

For all information, including to download brochures and application forms:

Visit
nsandi-adviser.com
Call us free on

* Fixed Interest Savings Certificates which matured before 8 October 2001, and have not been cashed-in or reinvested, earn the variable General Extension Rate at 0.09% pa from 1 April 2009 for each complete period of 3 months held.

2015/2016

CeMAP 1 Revision Guide

Offshore Deposits

- Applies to investments in banks based in other countries i.e. offshore.
- Known as a "tax haven" because they enjoy better tax rates.
- Popular offshore venues are countries where pound sterling is the currency so avoiding currency movements.
- Jersey, Isle of Mann are examples.
- Investor protection may be less than their UK counterpart.
- Investment income is taxable gross but will be liable to UK income tax usually when the money is brought back into the UK.

"ON EXCHANGE MARKETS TODAY, THE DOLLAR ROSE IN GERMANY, FELL IN JAPAN AND DISAPPEARED IN THE U.S.."

Money Market Instruments

Treasury Bills

- Short term redeemable securities.
- Issued by Debt Management Office (DMO).
- They are short term usually 91 days.
- They do not pay interest i.e. they are zero coupon.
- Profit is made by buying them at a discount to the redemption value.
- Low risk.
- Secondary market provided by banks – no market place.
- Held mainly by financial institutions seeking short term home for excess money.

Certificates of Deposit

- Short term larger scale funding.
- 3 to 6 months terms.
- £50,000 or more.
- Issued by banks and building societies.
- Interest paid along with repayment of capital.
- Bearer securities which allows the payment to be made to whoever bears the security, therefore can be sold before redemption.

Commercial Paper

- Issued by companies who want to raise money for working capital purposes as opposed to issuing corporate bonds.
- Large amounts issued.
- Purchasers being institutions such as pensions funds.
- Rates determined by credit rating of company.
- Issued between 5 to 45 days, on average these are 30 to 35 Days
- Companies with low credit rating can issue Commercial Paper if it is backed by a Letter of Credit from a bank.

CeMAP 1 Revision Guide

Fixed Interest Securities

- Bonds are one of the four main asset classes, the others being cash, shares and property. At its simplest, a bond is just a loan.
- If a government, company or financial institution wants to borrow some money, one of its options is to issue a bond.
- Typically, they'll pay interest (or a coupon) on a regular basis and then repay (or redeem) the full amount of the loan (the principal or nominal value) on a pre-determined date (the maturity date).
- Bonds, which are also known as fixed-income investments, are riskier than cash but less risky than property or shares.
- Consequently, over the long term, you'd expect bonds to return more than cash but less than property or shares.
- Investors can buy and sell bonds, through a broker, just like shares. The price of the bond depends on many factors.
- The term 'bond' is widely abused by the financial services industry. You may have heard of terms like 'savings bond', 'investment bond' and 'guaranteed equity bond'.

"OH LOOK, PAUL -- IT'S THE FIRST TIME SHE'S EVER PUT TWO WORDS TOGETHER!"

Government Gilts

- Gilts are bonds issued by the UK government. Most governments issue their own bonds.
- Most gilts pay a fixed rate of interest, known as the coupon, every six months but you can also get index-linked gilts where the interest paid and the final redemption amount rise in line with the rate of inflation.
- Gilts that are due to be redeemed within 7 years are known as 'shorts'. Those redeemed between 7 and 15 years hence are known as 'mediums' while those over 15 years are known as, believe it or not, 'longs'.
- The 0 to 7 year period comes from the Debt Management Office but the "press" commonly use 0 to 5 years
- Then there are some gilts which are undated, meaning that they have no redemption date.
- Gilts are usually sold in blocks of £100 nominal or par value. You will therefore see prices for them quoted in newspapers and on web sites at around this price.
- You'll see them listed as, for example, 8% Treasury 2022. The 8% is the rate of interest paid or coupon on each block of £100. Because rates are lower than this at moment, it will cost you more than £100 to buy this gilt today.
- 2022 is the redemption date. The word in the middle, such as 'Treasury' or 'Exchequer', is apparently to help differentiate one gilt from another.
- At the moment, the gilts market is worth in the region of £300b. So it is significantly smaller than the UK stock market, which is currently worth around £1,300B.

CeMAP 1 Revision Guide

Government Borrowing

Borrowing

Borrowing has fallen steeply after the Treasury reclaimed interest payments it made to the Bank of England. The central bank has become the Treasury's biggest lender following the purchase of almost a third of UK debt via its quantitative easing policy. Using the previous figures for borrowing, the annual deficit is expected to rise before it falls in 2014/15

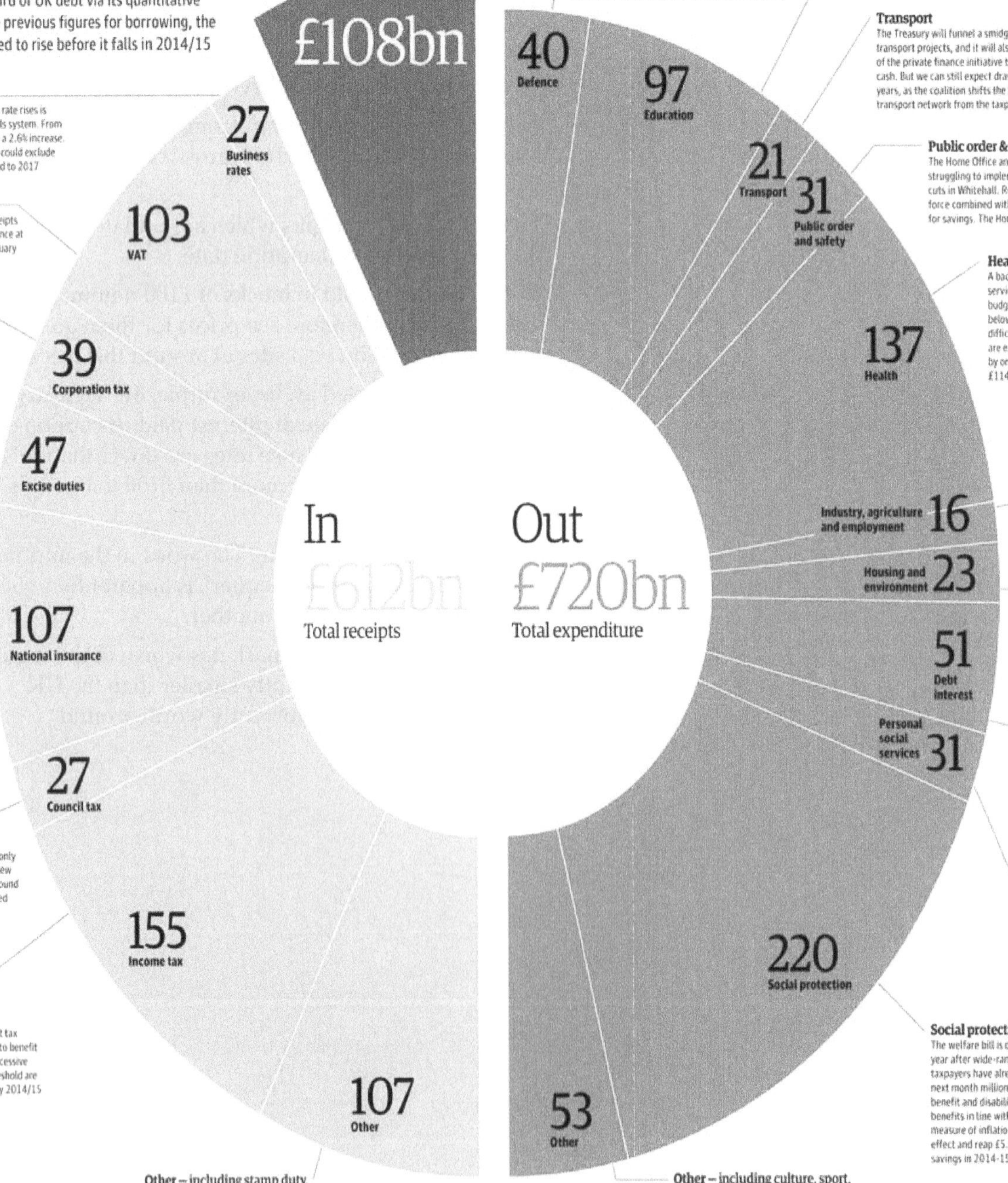

£108bn

In — £612bn Total receipts

Business rates — 27
Business groups say a series of steep rate rises is made worse by a bureaucratic appeals system. From April, the chancellor has pencilled in a 2.6% increase. A revaluation planned for 2015 that could exclude 300,000 businesses has been delayed to 2017

VAT — 103
The third biggest tax in terms of receipts, after income tax and national insurance at around £100bn. A rise to 20% in January 2011 brought in an extra £11.7bn.

Corporation tax — 39
Only worth about 9% of total tax receipts, corporation tax is due to decline further in value after the chancellor cut the current 24% rate to 20%, to take effect next year. The move will bring in £1bn a year less than if the rate had been kept at the 28% the coalition inherited in 2010

Excise duties — 47
Duties on beer and cigarettes have already gone up under this government. More rises are expected as the chancellor seeks to close the deficit

National insurance — 107
An emergency rise in national insurance in 2011, raising an extra £3bn a year, is not likely to be repeated after intense pressure from employers, despite rising unemployment restricting receipts to £102bn

Council tax — 27
There is much talk of changing the only tax on property, possibly creating new top-tier bands to capture million-pound homes. A two-year freeze has limited receipts to £26bn

Income tax — 155
The biggest element of government tax receipts, income tax was expected to benefit from a rise in employment. But successive rises in the personal allowance threshold are expected to cost an extra £3.9bn by 2014/15

Other — 107 — including stamp duty, vehicle excise duty
An expected rise in stamp duty receipts from share trades and house buying could pay for another freeze in fuel duty. A jump in petrol prices could force the government to abandon a planned rise in January

Out — £720bn Total expenditure

Defence — 40
According to the latest figures (2010), the UK is the fourth highest spender in cash terms on defence in the world behind the United States, China and France. But after fierce criticism of botched procurement and criticism of redundancies among serving soldiers, it has been partly protected from George Osborne's latest round of spending cuts, and will be allowed to roll over an underspend from this year, worth £1.6bn over the next two years

Education — 97
A capital budget of £7.2bn in 2010-11 that was due to bottom out at £3.3bn in 2013-14 will be partially restored. Around £4bn will be made available after April to create new school places and to carry out maintenance and repair work to existing school buildings. General spending will fall behind inflation

Transport — 21
The Treasury will funnel a smidgen more cash into major transport projects, and it will also use a new, souped-up version of the private finance initiative to try to attract private sector cash. But we can still expect drastic fare rises over the coming years, as the coalition shifts the burden for funding the transport network from the taxpayer to the passenger

Public order & safety — 31
The Home Office and Ministry of Justice are struggling to implement some of the steepest cuts in Whitehall. Redundancies in the police force combined with privatisations are key areas for savings. The Home Office is due a reprieve

Health — 137
A backstairs privatisation of the health service has eaten into hospital and GP budgets, which will make a small, below-inflation rise in spending this year difficult to manage. Below-inflation rises are expected to continue as the NHS gets by on £104bn in 2012-13, rising to £114bn in 2014/15

Industry, agriculture & employment — 16
The Department for Business, Innovation and Skills is expected to cut 15% from its spending over four years

Housing & environment — 23
House building has fallen to a record low. Not since the 1920s has the UK built so few homes. Nevertheless, it is an area targeted for cuts and environmental policy is likely to suffer most as green subsidies are rolled back

Debt interest — 51
Although the national debt has ballooned to more than £1 trillion, the UK is considered a safe haven by foreign lenders, which has kept interest rates low. That said, the UK must raise billions of pounds of new debt just to maintain spending

Personal social services — 31
A Cinderella area of spending, it covers home helps to social work and is a chief target for cuts. An ageing population is expected to put extra strain on budgets

Social protection — 220 — including tax credits
The welfare bill is one of the chief areas for cuts this year after wide-ranging cuts last year. Higher rate taxpayers have already lost their child benefit. From next month millions will lose tax credits, housing benefit and disability benefits. A switch to up-rating benefits in line with the lower consumer prices measure of inflation will have a cumulative savings effect and reap £5.8bn of the expected £11bn of savings in 2014-15

Other — 53 — including culture, sport, international development
Despite attacks from backbench Tory MPs, overseas aid spending is protected by the coalition government's commitment to raise overall expenditure in this area to the internationally agreed target of 0.7% of GDP

TEXT: PHILIP INMAN ECONOMICS CORRESPONDENT
GRAPHIC: GUARDIAN GRAPHICS, SOURCE: THE TREASURY
Figures rounded.

theguardian

52 — 2015/2016

Corporate Bonds

- Corporate bonds are bonds issued by a company. They can be split into two main classes.
- Bonds issued by large, reputable companies, such as GlaxoSmithKline and BAA, are referred to as investment grade bonds.
- Those issued by companies with less secure finances are known as non-investment grade, high yield or junk bonds.
- High yield bonds, as the name implies, offer a higher rate of interest than investment grade bonds.
- But there is a significant risk that the company may not be able to pay (or default) on the ongoing interest payments or redemption payment.
- As a group, high yield bonds tend to behave more like shares than gilt and investment grade bonds.
- Some companies issue convertible bonds. These are bonds that can be converted into shares at a later date.
- As they offer extra upside if the share price does well in the future, convertible bonds usually pay a lower rate of interest than non-convertible bonds.
- The UK corporate bond market is slightly smaller than the gilts market, currently being worth about £200B.

Local Authority Bonds

- Issued by local authorities to help fund their spending.
- Secured on local authority assets.
- Guaranteed returns, income paid half yearly, net of 20% tax.
- Not negotiable.
- On maturity the capital is returned.

Permanent Interest Bearing Shares (PIBS)

- Some building societies have issued bonds, known as permanent interest-bearing shares (PIBS).
- Unlike most bonds, PIBS have no fixed redemption date.
- If a building society were to go under, PIBS investors would only get their money after ordinary savings account holders got theirs.
- PIBS can be difficult to buy and sell as there is only a small market for many of those issued.
- In addition, you have to invest a minimum amount. This is usually £1,000 for the smaller building societies but can be up to £50,000.
- The market for PIBS is very small, currently being worth less than £1b.

Tax and Bonds

- The interest on gilts, corporate bonds and PIBs is subject to income tax although it is usually paid out without any income tax being deducted.
- Income from local authority bonds is paid net of 20%.
- You can put gilts, corporate bonds and PIBS into an ISA and thereby avoid paying any income tax on them.
- Any capital gains you make are free from tax.
- Unfortunately, you don't get any relief for capital losses.
- Unlike shares, you don't have to pay any stamp duty when you buy gilts, corporate bonds or PIBS.

Child Trust Fund

- A tax free savings account for children born since September 2002.
- Sponsored by the government but run by banks, building societies and other savings companies.
- The Coalition Government withdrew them in 2010 for all new investments and existing holders will no longer receive government injections.
- Here are some more facts that related to the product for existing holders.
  - Originally a £250 voucher was given to start each child's account by the government, this reduced to £50 in 2010, no new vouchers by January 2011.
  - Children in families receiving full Child Tax Credit received £500, reducing to £100 in 2010
  - Parents, family or friends can contribute £4,000 in the year between the child's birthdays.
  - Money cannot be taken out of the CTF once it has been put in – once your child is 18 they will be able to decide how to use the money.
  - Children can start to make decisions about how the money is managed when they are 16.
  - Not just one type of CTF account – you choose the type of account you want for your child – deposit based, shares based or stakeholder.
  - Stakeholder account invests in shares and has a maximum 1½% capped annual management charge.

"NO, I DON'T THINK MY SISTER'S IN HERE."

Annuities

- Provided by life assurance companies, who pay out a regular income for a specified period in exchange for a lump sum from a private individual or from a pension scheme. The person receiving the annuity is known as the annuitant.

Taxation

- Annuities resulting from Money Purchase Occupational or Stakeholder pensions are all taxed as earned income in the hands of the annuitant. Known as Compulsory Purchase Annuities.
- Annuities bought by clients with their own money (Purchased Life Annuities or PLAs) have a capital element which is deemed by the Inland Revenue to be a return of a portion of the purchase price, and is therefore not taxable.
- The remaining interest portion is taxable at the client's top rate, and PLAs are normally paid net of basic rate (20%) income tax on the interest portion.
- Immediate Needs Annuities, those bought with the proceeds of a Long Term Care plan and used to provide care, are tax free, so long as the payment is made direct to the care provider.

Interest rates and annuity rates

- Clients lock into the current long-term interest rates available when the annuity is purchased.
- Annuity rates increase when interest rates increase and vice versa.
- Once purchased, however, the amount of annuity is fixed and independent of interest rate changes.
- Most annuities are immediate annuities, i.e. they begin payment as soon as the purchase price is received. Deferred annuities begin payment after a specified period or at a fixed date or age.
- Most annuities are life annuities, related in some way to the survival of the annuitant. Only an annuity certain (now very rare) is paid for a fixed period with no reference to a life.

Financial Products

Types of Annuities

- Straightforward life annuities pay a level gross amount each month (or quarter, half year or year) until the death of the annuitant, or until the death of the survivor of two joint annuitants, without any return on death. There are, however, many varieties:

  - Escalating annuities provide income which increases by a fixed simple or compound rate of interest.

  - Guaranteed annuities (usually guaranteed for 5 years) ensure that payments are made for a minimum period even if the annuitant dies before that period finishes.

  - Capital protected annuities provide that if the annuitant dies before the total gross payments equal the purchase price, the balance is refunded in a lump sum.

  - Reversionary annuities provide an income which commences on the death of one individual and continues for the remaining lifetime of another individual.

  - Temporary annuities are payable for a specified term, but cease on the prior death of the annuitant.

  - With profit and unit linked annuities. The returns from these are linked to the performance of the underlying fund.

"The computer expert is here, sir."

Shares

Ordinary shares

- Holders of ordinary shares, or equities, are in effect part-owners of a company.
- Ordinary shares normally confer the right:
    - To receive a distribution of the companies' profits as dividends.
    - To have a say in the way the company is run, by voting at shareholders' meeting and electing a board of directors.
- Investment in shares may be by:
    - Purchasing them initially when a company Raises capital by issuing them, or
    - Buying them from existing shareholders on the stock market.
- Investment in shares cannot be cashed in by selling shares back to the company – they are sold to another investor on the stock market.
- The price of ordinary shares can go down as well as up, and depend on:
    - The profitability and dividends of the company.
    - Other economic and market forces.

Taxation

- Dividends are received net of 10%, with a tax credit.
    - Nil-rate taxpayers cannot reclaim;
    - Lower and basic rate payers have no further liability;
    - Higher rate payers owe a further amount to make the tax up to 32½% of the grossed-up dividend.
    - Additional rate payers will pay a total 37½ %
- Capital gains on shares are subject to CGT in the normal way.

Preference shares

- Preference shares, like ordinary shares, are entitled to dividends from the company's profits.
  - The dividends are often, but not necessarily, fixed. The dividends rank after payment of debenture interest etc., but ahead of ordinary share dividends.
- Preference shares also rank ahead of ordinary shares on the winding-up of a company, but behind loans.
- They therefore carry less risk than ordinary shares, but have less chance of high returns.

Convertible Shares

- Convertible shares carry the right to be converted later to ordinary shares of the issuing companies.
- Convertible share prices tend to follow the price trends of the shares to which they can be converted, but with less marked swings.

Rights Issues

- Stock Exchange rules require that when an existing company wishes to raise further capital by issuing more shares, those shares must first be offered to the existing shareholders.
- This is done by means of a Rights issue, offering for instance one new share per so many existing shares, possibly at a discount to the price at which the new shares are expected to commence trading.

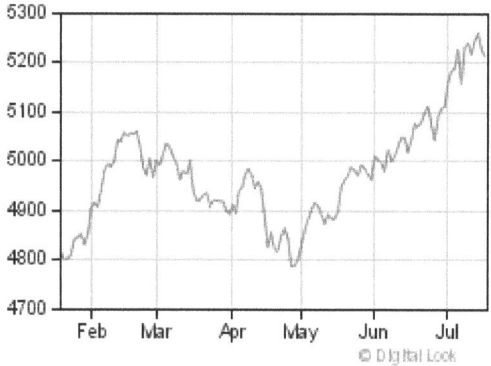

Earnings per share

- This is the amount of net profit divided by the number of shares.

Price/earnings ratio

- The returns from shares come from dividends and from growth in the share price. These two items are linked by the price/earnings or P/E ratio, which is calculated as the share price divided by the earnings per share.
- Shares with a relatively high P/E ratio are known as growth stocks, and the greater portion of the returns from them is likely to be obtained through increases in the share price.
- A ratio of 20 or more indicates a share is doing well

Dividend Cover

- A coverage ratio that measures a company's ability to pay off its required preferred dividend payments.
- A healthy company will have a high coverage ratio, indicating that it has little difficulty in paying off its preferred dividend requirements. Cover of 2.0 or more is considered healthy.

Loan Stocks and Debentures

- Owners of loan stocks effectively lend their money to companies.
- Interest is paid not dividends thus 20% tax deducted at source.
- Debentures are secured on company assets.
- Some allow conversion to ordinary shares.

"I'LL TELL YOU HOW SMART YOUR PORTFOLIO IS, RIGHT NOW IT'S VACATIONING IN SOUTHERN FRANCE."

Financial Products

Derivatives

Warrants

- Warrants give the holder the right to purchase a specified number of ordinary shares of the issuing company:
  - At a specified price.
  - On or between certain specified dates.
- They are high risk investments because, if the ordinary share price is less than the specified price on the specified dates, the warrant will not be exercised and therefore becomes valueless.
- Warrants do not receive dividends or interest.

Options

- An option is the right to buy or sell an investment (usually shares) at a specified price at a future date.
- An investor pays a price for the option and can choose whether to exercise the option (and hopefully make a profit on the share) or sell the option itself at a profit.
- Like warrants, these are high risk investments, as small changes in the share value can render the option valueless.

Futures

- These are similar to options except that there is an obligation to buy or sell at the specified price on the specified date.
- Futures are available in a variety of financial products as well as commodities, such as coffee, and even in currencies, where they can be used as a hedge against movements in exchange rates.
- Futures are also known as forward contracts. Forward Contracts are made directly between two parties and not traded

Why is Mike Ashley buying Tesco shares?

Nils Pratley
The Guardian

Mike Ashley, the billionaire Sports Direct chief, has made a £43m "investment" in Tesco, to reflect his "belief" in the troubled supermarket's "long-term future". Fine words, says Nils Pratley, but they merely dress up "a straightforward punt" – and it is Sports Direct's investors whose cash is on the line. Ashley has agreed a "put option" with Goldman Sachs to buy 23 million Tesco shares at a set price in the future. There's certainly an argument that despite its travails, Tesco's shares – now half the price they were a year ago – "represent decent value". But Ashley's "punting record does not inspire confidence": he lost a large sum gambling on a recovery at the doomed HBOS. At least then he was risking his own money; he now seems to think that owning 58% of Sports Direct gives him "the right to use the business as a vehicle for speculation". Losing the maximum £43m wouldn't cripple a company worth almost £4bn. But what is the limit on these gambles? At what level will Sports Direct's "supine" board "tell Ashley to use his own cash if he fancies a flutter"?

Structured Products

- These offer a guarantee of original capital with exceptional interest returns and have been actively marketed by firms to investors looking for high returns
- They have been popular with normal consumers who don't understand the complexities of the product and as a result, the FCA have issued some intense guidelines to firms.
- The main premise of structured products is that you receive a guaranteed amount of income with your capital safe, except where certain parameters fall out of place e.g., markets fall dramatically, indices fall. The guarantees can sometimes be provided by the use of derivatives which put the fear of god into some people Hence they are misunderstood by the average consumer
- There are 3 types:
    - Structured deposits – gives interest returns which may vary around the performance of shares or indices or other parameters
    - Structured Capital at Risk Product – SCARPs – these are products where both the income and capital can vary against parameters.
    - Non SCARP Product – where the capital is guaranteed except where share firm goes bust. Derivatives ensure this promise

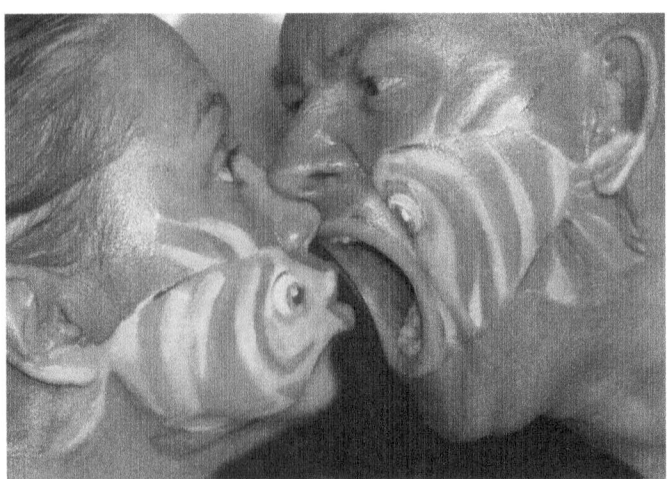

Financial Products

Enterprise Investment Schemes

- Enterprise Investment Schemes (EIS) were introduced by the government to encourage investment in small unquoted companies. Typically they involve a higher degree of risk than investments in larger companies, such as those traded on the London Stock Exchange.
- They can give you the following tax reliefs:
  - 30% upfront income tax relief on investments up to a £1 million for the current tax year and/or £1 million carried back to the previous tax year, as long as you keep their EIS shares for at least three years
  - 100% inheritance tax relief after two years, provided you still have your EIS shares at the time of your death
  - Capital gains tax deferral for the life of your investment
  - Tax-free growth, provided you qualify for income tax relief
- Remember you have to hold your EIS shares for a minimum of three years

Venture Capital Trusts (VCTs)

- VCTs are listed in the London Stock Exchange and provide finance for small, expanding companies with the aim of generating returns for investors. They're a tax-efficient way to invest in smaller companies. You can benefit from:
  - up to 30% income tax relief, if you invest between £5,000 and £200,000 in any tax year (to retain this relief you have to keep your VCT shares for at least five years).
  - tax-free dividends
  - no capital gains tax

Stock Markets

The Stock Exchange

- A full listing on the Stock Exchange is available only to those (usually very large) companies who can meet the stringent financial and other requirements laid down in the Exchange's rule book. In addition:
  - They must have been trading for at least 3 years.
  - At least 25% of their share capital must be in public hands.

The Alternative Investment Market (AIM)

- This market commenced trading in 1995, and is intended for new smaller companies with potential for growth.
- It effectively replaced the Unlisted Securities Market (USM), which ceased trading in 1996.
- Rules are less strict than for the Stock Exchange.
- Investment in companies on the AIM should be considered higher risk.
- The benefit of access to public finance and an enhancement of the company's profile are advantages of a listing.

Off Market Trading

- Known as over the market trading or dark pools.
- Common with large institutions trading large blocks of shares outside of the markets

Investing in shares

- An investor buys (or sells) shares through a stockbroker.
- The broker acts in effect as a middle-man, charging a fee for his services.
- The broker obtains the shares from market makers, who are in effect, the wholesalers of stocks.
- They make their profits by trading in stocks and shares.

Real Estate

Residential Property Investment

- Residential property investment is the growth area for private individual fuelled by Buy to Let mortgages.
  - ➢ Advantages include good rental yields and a mature market.
  - ➢ Disadvantages include prices can fall as well as rise and large upfront costs.
- Income tax is due on the letting income, subject to any allowable deductions, such as mortgage interest, repair, and replacement and maintenance costs.
- A house, which is an only or main residence and has been throughout the period of ownership, is exempt from capital gains tax when it is sold.
- Property, which is not your main residence, is liable for Capital Gains Tax.
- The greatest risk with Buy to Let is being unable to find a suitable tenant.

Commercial Property

- Commercial property includes:
  - ➢ Offices.
  - ➢ Individual retail shops.
  - ➢ Shopping malls and shopping centres.
  - ➢ Industrial units, i.e. factories, workshops.
  - ➢ Hotels and leisure resorts.
- Commercial property provides high rental income together with steady growth in capital value.
- The main advantages are:
  - ➢ Regular rent reviews.
  - ➢ Long leases.
  - ➢ Stable and longer-term tenants
- Commercial property does not show spectacular growth in value .
- Interest rates on borrowing for commercial property may be higher than for residential loans.

Real Estate Investment Trusts

- From 1st January 2007, listed UK Companies can elect to join the UK Real Estate Investment Trust (REIT) regime.
- The benefit to them is that any income or gains from their investment properties contained in the REIT are exempt from Corporation Tax.
- This creates a very exciting investment opportunity for people, like you and I, who have smaller amounts but would like to invest in a range of properties.
- For individuals wanting to invest in property in a tax efficient manner, the REIT is ideal, and also avoids many of the disadvantages of direct property investment.
- Income from the REIT will be treated as UK Property Income with 22% deducted at source. They are not dividends.
- No one individual can hold more than 10% of the value of the REIT.
- At least 75% of gross income must come from rent and at least 75% of its assets must be investment property.
- At least 90% of net profits must be distributed to shareholders.
- No individual shareholder can hold more than 10% of the shares and they can be held in ISAs, JISA's and child trust funds, SIPPs.

Commodities

- Traditional trading in gold, silver, foodstuffs.
- Nowadays big business in electricity, gas, internet bandwidth.
- Forward contracts allow you to secure prices for your commodity at times in the future.
- Helps companies even out raw material prices.
- For example the Kenco Coffee Company buys all its coffee beans on the forward market and is able to even out the wild fluctuations in bean prices so that the price of a jar of coffee remains fairly stable.

"WHY CAN'T YOU TALK TO YOUR PLANTS LIKE OTHER PEOPLE?!"

Foreign Exchange

- With countries people use their own currencies to purchase goods and services.
- Sterling in the UK, dollar in the US, Euro in Europe.
- When a person or company buys goods from abroad, they must use that country's currency to secure the transaction.
- They would need to obtain the relevant currency usually by using their bank to "buy" this currency from the foreign exchange markets.
- The foreign exchange market is a 24/7 market relying totally on technology to operate from all over the market.
- As with any market, prices of different currencies will vary with demand. For example if there is a big demand for people to buy US Dollars, this will increase the price. In other words you will need more of your currency to buy US Dollars.
- Thus, we get currency fluctuations.
- Currency speculators are traders who make a living buying and selling currency.
- Just like property speculators who make money buying and selling property and just like car dealers who do the same.

Unit trusts

- Unit trusts are collective investments established under a trust deed.
- Trustees oversee the running of unit trusts.
- They are unitised funds, with each unit representing a proportion of the fund's total asset value.
- Unit prices rise or fall, directly reflecting the value of the underlying assets.
- Investments are made by buying units from the unit trust managers (either directly or via an adviser) at the offer price, and cashed in by selling them back to the managers at the bid price.
- Units are not traded on the Stock Exchange.
- Historic pricing is based on the price the night before. Nowadays forward pricing or real time pricing is used to reflect the most up to date unit price.
- Income received by managers on the underlying investments is normally distributed to unit holders.
- Accumulation units aim to re-invest the dividends back into the fund by allocating you more units instead of cash.
- Some unit trusts aim for high income distributions, some for capital growth, and some for a balance of the two.
- Charges are:
  - An initial charge of 5%-6% in the bid/offer spread.
  - An annual management fee of between 0.5% and 2% of the value of the fund.
- Taxation within the fund.
  - Fund managers are subject to tax on their income but not on capital gains. CGT is liable for the unit holders.
- Distributions.
  - Distributions are received by investors net of 10% with a tax credit. Nil-rate taxpayers cannot reclaim it. Lower rate and basic rate taxpayers have no further liability.
  - Higher rate taxpayers owe a further amount to make the tax up to 32½% of the grossed up distribution.
  - 37½ % for Additional Rate Taxpayers
- Investors are liable for CGT in the normal way.

Non-mainstream pooled investments

- As the name suggests, these are the exception. They are pooled investments that don't adhere to the FCAs rules on pooled investments.
- The FCA authorises these types of investments and they are therefore allowed to be sold in the UK. We're typically talking about unit trusts and OEICs.
- The non-mainstream investments, unit trusts, traded life policies and such, have more investment freedom, with providers based abroad and very little investor protection.
- The FCA doesn't deem them suitable to retail investors and doesn't allow them to be marketed accordingly.

"NO TRICKS!"

Investment Trusts

- Investment Trusts are collective investments, but they are NOT unitised funds like unit trusts.
- They are public limited companies whose business is investing in stocks and shares of other companies (They are not trusts!).
- Investment in an investment trust is made by buying and selling its shares on the stock market.
- Investment trust share prices are affected not only by the underlying value of the company's assets (as with unit trusts) but also by other market forces.
- The share price can sometimes therefore stand at a discount to the asset value.
- Charges tend to be lower than those for unit trusts.
- As public companies, investment trusts (unlike unit trusts) are able to benefit from "gearing", i.e. they can also borrow in order to further their investment aims, so they have greater flexibility to make use of opportunities.
- Split-capital investment trusts allow investors to have all of the income or all of the capital rather than having smaller amounts of both.

"This is Hoggets, he's worked here for about five years although he's been with us for twenty."

Open ended investment companies (OEICs)

- Open ended investment companies (OEICs) are a form of pooled investment which is popular in Europe.

- Under UK regulations, unit trusts are able to convert into OEIC's.

- Investors buy participating redeemable preference shares in the company, which can issue an unlimited number of shares. Shares are traded at a single price (i.e. there is no bid-offer spread), but initial charges will be taken.

- "Umbrella" funds are common, in which the company invests in a variety of types of shares.

- New funds can easily be created, and switches between funds are straightforward.

- The Depositary oversees the OEIC and is similar to the trustee in a Unit Trust.

- An Authorised Corporate Director manages the investments and buys and sells shares.

"A rise is out of the question Potts, but I'll let you sit in my chair for ten minutes."

New Individual Savings Accounts ISAs

- A government backed savings initiative for the masses, giving tax reliefs.
- Maximum annual investment £15,000.

Equity ISA

- Includes shares, unit trusts, Gilts, OEICs, Investment Trusts, REITS and Child Tax Funds.
- Minimum age 18.
- No CGT or income tax on dividends, although the 10% deducted on dividends cannot be reclaimed
- The maximum investment in 2015/16 is £15,240.
- Individuals can invest in any combination of cash and/or stocks and shares ISA

Cash ISA

- Building Society, Bank Accounts and National Savings.
- Minimum age 16.
- Tax free interest.

General features

- Withdrawals at any time, although you have to use your annual allowance to make further investments.
- You can have cash or equity elements from the same provider or different ones.

Junior ISA

- Available to children under age 18 who didn't qualify for the Child Trust Fund therefore no government contribution
- Anyone – family, friends – can contribute up to £4,080 per annum
- Invested in cash or equities in a similar manner to ISA
- Income tax free but no withdrawals until aged 18

CeMAP 1 Revision Guide

Help to Buy ISA

If you're a first time buyer, save up to £200 a month towards your first home with a Help to Buy ISA and the government will boost your savings by 25%. That's a £50 bonus for every £200 you save. You can receive a bonus of up to £3,000.

- new accounts will be available for 4 years, but once you have opened an account there's no limit on how you long you can save for
- accounts will be available through banks and building societies from Autumn 2015
- you can make an initial deposit of £1,000 when you open the account – in addition to normal monthly savings
- there is no minimum monthly deposit – but you can save up to £200 a month
- accounts are limited to one per person rather than one per home – so those buying together can both receive a bonus
- only available to individuals who are 16 and over
- the bonus is available to first time buyers purchasing UK properties
- minimum bonus size of £400 per person
- maximum bonus size of £3,000 per person
- the bonus will be available on home purchases of up to £450,000 in London and up to £250,000 outside London
- the bonus will be paid when you buy your first home

If you save £12,000, the government bonus will boost your total savings to £15,000.

74   2015/2016

Endowment Assurance

Non-profit endowment

- Fixed premium for a fixed (guaranteed) sum assured on death or at the end of the term.
- Very few investment policies are now issued on this basis.

With-profit endowment

- For a higher fixed premium, the policyholder gets not just a guaranteed minimum sum assured, but also a chance to share in the company's profits, by means of added bonuses.
- Reversionary bonuses:
    - Normally added annually, and, once added, cannot be removed.
    - May be simple (based on the sum assured) or compound (based on the sum assured and previously-added bonuses).
- Terminal bonuses:
    - Added only at the point of claim, on death or maturity.
    - The rate can be increased or reduced to reflect the success or otherwise of stock market investment by the company.
- Neither reversionary or terminal bonuses are guaranteed to be added

Principles and Practices of Financial Management

- Sets out how a firm manages it's with profits business.
    - Annual certification to FCA that adhering to document
    - Customer friendly document o be made available.

Low cost with-profit endowment

- The guaranteed sum assured is set at such a level that the bonuses expected to be added would be sufficient to raise the claim value to a certain level after a specified period.
- This is normally used for mortgage purposes, with the aim being that the final claim value should be equal to the mortgage amount.
- Additional life cover is added so that the death claim value is always at least equal to the projected final value.

Unit-linked Endowments

- Unit-linked endowments are suitable for investors who:

    ➤ Prefer a more direct link to stock-market type investments;

    ➤ Are willing to accept more investment risk (without guarantees) for the chance of making greater gains;

    ➤ Wish to have control over the particular type of investments for their policy.

- Premiums paid are (possibly after the deduction of certain expenses) allocated to purchase units in a chosen fund or funds at the appropriate offer price.

- A pool of units builds up and these units are cashed in at the appropriate bid price to:

    ➤ Pay the ongoing expenses of running the policy as described in the policy details;

    ➤ Pay the costs of providing any life/sickness cover which the policy provides;

    ➤ Pay out the surrender, maturity, or death claim value when the policy ceases.

- The level of charges to cover expenses is much more visible on unit-linked policies than on with-profits policies. They may include some or all of the following:

    ➤ The bid-offer spread on the price of units;

    ➤ A regular monthly policy fee;

    ➤ An initial nil-allocation period during which premiums are not allocated to purchase units;

    ➤ An initial period in which the units purchased are "capital units", which suffer higher annual charges than the normal units (and therefore are slower to increase in value).

Unitised with-profit endowments

- This product is suitable for clients who like the guarantees provided by with profits policies, but who would like to explore the possibility of changing the risk profile of the investment element of the policy.
- The concept of unitised with-profits lies somewhere between with profits and unit-linked.
- The pricing structure is similar to that of unit-linked policies, except that management charges are not explicit.
- As with traditional with profit policies, unitised with profits contracts are entitled to bonuses which depend on the performance of the company's life fund:
  - Bonuses are added either by increasing the unit price or by allocating additional units to the policy.
  - Once added, bonuses cannot be taken away - i.e. unit prices cannot fall except in the case of surrender (see below).
- Unitised with-profit policies give a guaranteed minimum amount payable on death or maturity.
- This amount is usually based on a minimum annual percentage rate of growth on units of the unitised with profits fund.
- If the unit value is greater than this, the larger amount is paid.
- However, on surrender, a deduction can be made from the bid value of the units, to allow for the investment conditions at the time.
- This is called the Market Value Adjustment, or MVA.

Qualifying Policies

- An endowment policy has special tax advantages.
- The funds grow and tax is deducted at source. This tax is equivalent to basic rate tax and capital gains tax.
- No further high rate tax is deducted from the gains made so long as the policy is "qualifying".
- Policies are "qualifying" provided they do not break anyone or more of the following rules:
  - Ten-year rule: premiums must be payable annually or more frequently, for at least 10 years (some term assurances are exempt from this rule).
  - Two-times rule: premiums in anyone year must not exceed twice the premiums in any other year.
  - Premiums must be paid regularly. At least annually.
  - One-eighth rule: premiums in any one year must not exceed one eighth of the total premiums due to be paid in the policy.
  - 75% rule: the sum assured on death must never be less than 75% of the total premiums due to be paid on the policy (or, for whole of life policies, 75% of the total premiums due before the 75th birthday).
  - Qualifying policies are treated as non-qualifying if surrendered or made paid up within 10 years, or ¾ of term if less.
  - Since 2012, qualifying endowments premiums cannot exceed £3,600 per annum

Investment Bonds

- Investment Bonds are collective investment vehicles based on unitised funds.
- They are unit-linked, single premium, non-qualifying whole of life policies.
- Investment is achieved by paying a single premium for the policy.
- The single premium nominally purchases units in a specified fund or funds and the subsequent value of the policy is based on the value of these units (although, unlike unit trust unit-holders, the policyholder does not actually own the units).
- The investment is cashed in by surrendering the policy for a value equal to the bid value of the units nominally attaching to the policy.
- On death, the policy ceases and a slightly enhanced value (often 101% of the bid value) is paid out.
- Switching from one fund to another is often allowed without charging the bid-offer spread.
- A form of "income" can be taken by making regular withdrawals (small partial surrenders made by cashing in units).
- These withdrawals are tax-free to basic rate taxpayers, and up to 5% p.a. of the original investment may be withdrawn each year (up to a total of 100%) without incurring an immediate tax liability, even for higher rate taxpayers.
- Unused 5% allowances can be carried forward.
- A tax liability may arise on death, maturity, encashment, part encashment or assignment for money. The system of calculating any tax due is known as "Top Slicing"

Taxation

- Gains in the underlying funds are charged to tax which eliminates any liability for basic rate tax and capital gains tax for individuals.
- Neither is recoverable by policyholders who are not taxpayers.
- An additional charge of 20% tax is incurred by higher rate taxpayers on encashment of the Bond. 25% for Additional Rate Taxpayers.

"IF I KNEW WHEN THE STOCK MARKET WAS GOING UP, WOULD I BE SITTING HERE ANSWERING STUPID QUESTIONS?"

Life Assurance Policies

- The sum assured is payable only if the life assured dies within a specified period.
- Premiums are normally level, even when the sum assured varies from year to year.
- There is no maturity value and no surrender value at any time.
- There is no return of premiums if the life assured survives the specified term.
- The term can be anything from a few months to 40 years or more, but if the expiry date is after age 65, it may be better to take a whole of life assurance.

Level Term Assurance

- Sum assured remains level throughout; therefore real value may be eroded by inflation.
- Level annual/monthly premiums or single premium.
- Uses – family protection, key person insurance, cover for loans, debts.

"FIRST, THE GOOD NEWS IS YOU'LL SOON STOP HAVING COLDS!"

Pension Term Assurance

- "A" Day for pensions (April 2006) brought in lots of new legislation for the pensions industry.
- One of the results was that virtually anyone could have a Pension Term Assurance and get substantial tax reliefs on their monthly premiums.
- Pension Term Assurance is virtually the same as level term assurance except you can get up to 45% tax relief on the premiums.
- In December 2006, the Government spotted this loophole and blocked it.
- Policies written on or before 6th December 2006 still attract tax relief at the policyholder's highest marginal rate.

Decreasing Term Assurance

- Commonly used to cover loans such as mortgages or hire purchase.
- The sum assured decreases over the term, either:
    - By equal monthly or annual amounts;
    - By irregular amounts;
    - For example, to cover the reducing inheritance tax liability due to the tapering relief provisions for a Potentially Exempt Transfer;
    - In line with the reduction of the capital outstanding on a repayment mortgage at a specified rate of interest (often known as a mortgage protection policy).
- Can be single life policies, or joint life first death.
- Premiums are lower than for level term assurance.
- Premiums are level even though the sum assured reduces.

Gift Inter Vivos

- Rather fancy name for a decreasing term assurance to cover the IHT liability left from a Potentially Exempt Transfer (PET).
- 7 year term assurance altogether. 3 years level and then drops by 20% each year for 4 years, just like the liability of a PET.
- The policy is put into trust for the person who will have to pay the liability.

Family Income Benefit (FIB)

- On the death of the life assured within the policy term, the company will pay out a series of payments (usually quarterly or monthly) from the date of death until the end of the policy term.
- This method is suitable for dependants who might have difficulty in coping with a lump sum, and might spend it all at once, leaving themselves nothing to live on later.
- The payments are treated as instalments of capital, and are therefore not subject to income tax.
- The payments can be commuted into a lump sum, which would be less than the total of the outstanding instalments.

Convertible

- Life cover is the same as normal term assurance.
- Contains option to convert to permanent policy (whole life or endowment) for up to the same sum assured without further medical evidence.
- Premium after conversion is the standard rate for the age at conversion.
- Useful for people who:
    - Want to begin a policy taking advantage of current good health;
    - Want a more permanent contract but cannot afford the premiums yet.

Renewable

- Typically 5 or 10-year policies.
- They can be renewed at the end of the term without further evidence of health, i.e. a similar policy is issued for the same sum assured, but the premium is now that for the age at renewal.
- Again, useful for those wishing to keep initial premiums to a minimum.

Increasable

- The option exists, without evidence of health, to increase the cover on a specified date or dates, or when extending the term under a renewability option as described above.

Whole of Life assurance policies

Features

- Pays out policy benefits on the death of the life assured whenever that death occurs.
- Single life or joint lives (first or second death).
- Premiums can be payable throughout life or limited to a chosen age or term. Acquires a surrender value -but it is not an investment policy.

With-profit Whole of Life

- Guaranteed minimum death benefit (sum assured) plus a share of the investment profits of the life fund.
- Level premium, greater than for without-profit policy with same sum assured.
- Reversionary bonuses.
  - Declared annually (usually) as an addition to the amount payable on death.
  - Quoted as a simple or compound percentage of the sum assured.
  - Once declared, cannot be removed.
- Terminal bonuses.
  - Allow for rises and falls in the fund's stock market investments. Added only in the event of a claim.
  - Rates vary from time to time.
- Interim bonuses.
- Reversionary bonuses added to a claim arising between bonus declaration dates.

Unit-linked (or flexible) whole of life assurance

- Policy returns are not guaranteed, but depend on fund performance.
- Premiums buy units at the offer price.
- The cost of policy benefits and the charges of running the policy are met by cashing units in at the bid price.
- Different funds are available to meet the needs of people with very different risk profiles.
- Policies are very flexible and allow for different levels of cover to be chosen for the same premium amount:
  - ➢ Minimum cover: low protection amount and policy builds up an investment reserve (not recommended as a pure investment policy).
  - ➢ Balanced cover: the amount of protection expected to be maintained throughout life by that premium level, based on a stated assumed growth rate (usually around 7% or 8%).
  - ➢ Maximum cover: cover guaranteed to be maintained for a stated time (often 10 years), but unlikely to be sustained beyond that on assumed growth rates - similar to a term assurance and often cheaper.
- The level of cover can be changed (increases require underwriting).
- The initial cover level is often guaranteed for 10 years. Thereafter, policies contain regular review dates, with the opportunity to increase premiums or reduce cover if growth rate has not matched assumptions.
- A wide range of other benefits in addition to life cover can be added and paid for by cashing units at bid price e.g. critical illness, sickness cover. In that case it may be called universal whole of life.

Joint Life 2nd Death

- Usually a whole of life policy in joint names will pay out when the first person dies.
- 2nd death is where the second person has to die before the sum assured is paid out.
- These are ideal to provide a lump sum in the event of spouses both dying and leaving an IHT liability to be paid.
- The policy is put in trust for the beneficiaries so they receive it immediately and pay off the IHT liability.

Income Protection Insurance

- IPI also known as Permanent Health provides an income during disability caused by sickness or injury. It is available to employees and the self-employed.
- 'Permanent' means that the policy cannot be cancelled by the company.
- Deferred period (usually 4, 13, 26, 52 weeks) must elapse from start of disability before benefits begin.
- Benefits are then paid until recovery, retirement or death.
- Disability is defined in terms of being unable to work (a typical definition might be: unable to follow own occupation or any other for which suited by training/experience).
  - Some companies offer limited benefits to housewives.
  - Proportionate benefit may be payable if a lower-paid job is taken due to disability.
- Maximum benefit usually 50% to 75% of income and providers at the top end of the scale may deduct state benefits.
- Protection is for a chosen term ending at or before state retirement age.
- Premium levels are higher for some occupations.
- Policies can be pure protection or on a unit-linked basis Benefits are tax-free for policies effected by individuals.
- Types of premiums
  - Reviewable – increase over the term
  - Renewable – renewed periodically according to market risks at the time
  - Guaranteed – remain the same

Taxation

- Individual plans are tax free
- Company sponsored plans are taxable as earned income when the employee receives the income but most are not treated as a benefit in kind although they are charged as a tax deductible business expense

Financial Products

Critical Illness Cover

- Unlike PHI/IPI, this pays a lump sum (not income) on the diagnosis of one of a number of specified illnesses/conditions.
- Payment of the sum assured is not delayed until death from the illness.
- The list of illnesses usually includes: heart attack, cancer, stroke, coronary artery surgery, kidney failure, major organ transplant, total and permanent disability (but not AIDS).
- Uses of the lump sum:
    - To help make the sufferer's last days/years more pleasant.
    - To enable them to move to more convenient accommodation.
    - To repay the mortgage in part or in full.
    - To pay for medical treatment,

"THAT, JASON, IS THE AURA OF MONEY!"

Private Medical Insurance

- Private Medical Insurance provides cover for individuals who wish to use private medical treatment facilities rather than the National Health Service, in order to:
    - Speed up access to treatment.
    - Obtain freedom of choice of hospital and consultant obtain access to treatment not available on the NHS.
- Cover normally includes:
    - Hospital charges.
    - Specialists' fees.
    - Surgery.
    - Nursing care.
    - In-patient or out-patient facilities may be included.
- The cost depends on several factors, including:
    - The range of treatment covered.
    - The choice of hospitals.
- Tax relief on premiums for those over 60 was abolished from 2nd July 1997.
- Some employers provide this cover for employees free or at a reduced rate. If so, the premiums paid for the employee are taxed as a benefit in kind.

General Protection

- The following products, which are similar in nature to life assurance products, or are sold in conjunction with life products, are provided by general insurance companies:

Personal Accident and Sickness Insurance

- Renewable annually – company can cancel.
- A lump sum is paid on death, loss of one or both eyes, loss of one or more limbs, or permanent total inability to work again.
- May also include cover for temporary disablement or medical expenses.
- No tax relief on premiums.
- Benefits are tax-free.

Accident, Sickness and Unemployment

- Bought alongside a mortgage with cover linked to the mortgage and associated cost monthly repayment.
- Cover normally payable for one or two years maximum.

Long Term Care Insurance

- This product provides funds to meet cost of care.
- The amount of benefit paid is determined by the need of the policy holder and how many ADLs (Activities of Daily Living) they can't do.
- Examples of ADLs are washing, feeding, dressing, preparing food and using the toilet.
- Benefits are tax free provided an immediate needs annuity is purchased

Business Protection Insurance

Features

- The main aim is to protect businesses against the financial consequences of the death or disability of a partner, or director, or important employee.
- The type of cover used could be whole life, term assurance, critical illness or permanent health insurance as appropriate.
- The aim is to enable surviving partners to purchase a deceased partner's share of the business. This is done with life assurance policies, the precise means being determined by the terms of an agreement between the partners.
- There are three basic types of agreement which may be used.

Automatic accrual

- The deceased partner's share is automatically shared among the survivors (i.e. it does not pass to the beneficiaries of the deceased's estate).
- Each partner is obliged to insure his own life, and the proceeds of this policy, written in trust for his family, compensate the family for the loss of the share of the business.
- There is no IHT on the proceeds (in trust); premiums are technically PETs, but should avoid IHT due to the "normal expenditure" exemption provisions.

Buy and sell agreement

- This binds the deceased partner's estate to sell his share of the business, and binds the surviving partners to buy it.
- Each partner affects a life policy to the value of his share, in trust for the other partners. This provides the funds to buyout his share on his death.
- Because it is a binding contract for sale, the deceased's family are deemed to receive cash rather than business assets, and business property relief from IHT is not available.

Cross option agreement

- Similar to "Buy and Sell", except that each party has the option of insisting that the sale to the surviving partners takes place within a specified time.
- In practice the sale always takes place, but because it is only an option, business property relief is still allowed.

"HELLO - IS THIS THE LAW FIRM OF GRISBY, MARKS, AND CHADWICK?"

General Insurance

Indemnity

- A principle that shows how general insurance differs from life assurance.
- Covers you in the event of a financial loss and indemnifies you for this loss so you are restored to your previous position.
- Indemnity is given in cash terms, repair (e.g. car insurance), replacement (e.g. video players being stolen or reinstatement (e.g. buildings insurance).

Average

- This principle ensures people insure their potential loss for the right amount of cover.
- For example the total value of your contents might be £40,000 but you've only insured yourself for £20,000.
- In the event of any claim, the amount paid out would be half of your claim since you were only insured for half in the first place.

Excess

- To deter small claims, policies have excesses imposed which is a sum held back from your claim.

Buildings Insurance

- Standard cover on a property insurance typically includes the following:
    - Fire, explosion, lightning, earthquake;
    - Storm and flood;
    - Subsidence;
    - Escape of water, oil or frost damage;
    - Riot and civil commotion;
    - Malicious damage;
    - Impact by falling trees, aircraft, vehicles, animals.

Contents Insurance

- Provides cover for moveable items in a property against the same perils as above.
- Also can include accidental damage to contents.
- All risks cover protects your personal items, such as jewellery and digital cameras when you take them outside of your home.

"IT'S SIMPLE... YOU TURN OVER YOUR ENTIRE BANK ACCOUNT AND WE, IN TURN, GIVE YOU THE BEST COVERAGE MONEY CAN BUY!"

Private Motor Insurance

- Third Party.
  - The Road Traffic Act 1988 makes this cover compulsory.
  - Covers death or injury to third parties, damage to property and legal costs.
- Third Party, fire and theft.
  - Also covers fire damage to your car and theft.
- Comprehensive.
  - Adds the benefits of accidental damage to your car, loss of personal items and windscreen damage.

Travel Insurance

- Provides cover for holiday trips in event of:
  - Cancellation.
  - Missed flights.
  - Medical expenses.
  - Legal expenses.

Mortgages

- Many people think the mortgage is the loan but it is merely the security for the loan.
- It is a legal contract that enables a borrower to offer a property as security for a loan, thus enabling ownership of the property to be acquired.
- The mortgage is the Legal Charge or Mortgage Deed agreed between the two parties, the lender and the borrower. The Mortgage is the security for the loan and gives the lender powers over the property whilst the loan is outstanding.
- The two parties to a mortgage are:
    - The borrower, known as the mortgagor.
    - The lender, known as the mortgagee.

Types of Mortgage

Repayment mortgage

- Monthly repayments to the lender consist of interest charged on the amount borrowed, and also an element of capital repayment.
- The capital outstanding decreases, slowly at first and then more quickly, until it is fully repaid at the end of the term.
- The interest content of the repayment gradually decreases.
- If interest rates rise, the monthly repayment increases, and vice versa.
- The loan is guaranteed to be repaid at the end of the term, subject to all the correct repayments having been made.
- An advantage to lenders of the repayment mortgage is that the capital which is repaid each month is available to use for new loans.

Interest only mortgage

- The borrower pays only the interest each month to the lender, the agreement being to repay the capital in full at the end of the term.
- Since no capital is repaid until the end, the interest payments remain unchanged throughout, except of course that they change when rates of interest change.
- Borrowers usually arrange to repay the lump sum by means of an investment vehicle such as a life policy, or the tax-free cash from a stakeholder pension.
- If the repayment vehicle is a life policy, lenders often insist on it being assigned to them, although some choose not to because of the extra administration involved.
- Under the Mortgage Market Review, lenders must obtain evidence that the borrower has a credible repayment plan in force.

Mortgage Payment Vehicles

Endowment Policies

- The most common types of endowments for mortgage purposes are the low-cost with profits version and the unit-linked policy.
- The low-cost policy is made up of:
    - A with-profit endowment on which the estimated maturity value (based on a conservative reversionary bonus rate, and not allowing for terminal bonus) will repay the loan at the end of the term.
    - A term assurance (possibly decreasing term) to ensure repayment of the full loan if death occurs before the sum assured plus bonuses have reached the loan amount.
- The unit-linked policy is made up of:
    - A unit-linked endowment which would repay the loan at the end of the term on a stated assumed growth rate (with regular reviews to help keep fund growth on target).
    - A term assurance (as above) to cover early death.
- There is no guarantee that the required value will be reached.
- Problems can occur if interest and/or premium payments cannot be maintained – endowments are unlikely to have any surrender value in the first few years, and this can make worse a situation where a forced sale at a low price leaves a borrower in debt to the lender.
- If the bonuses or the growth rate on the policy exceed those assumed in the premium calculations, the policy will produce more than required to repay the loan, and the borrower will receive the surplus.

Personal/Stakeholder Pensions

- Personal pension are covered in more detail at the end of this chapter.
- The mortgage is repaid out of the 25% tax-free cash.
- Unlike the endowment mortgage, pension contributions obtain the benefit of tax relief, and the investment grows virtually tax-free.
- Additional life cover is required on a level basis to protect against the death of the borrower before the loan is repaid.

ISA

- Repayment of the loan is through regular and continuing (usually monthly) payments into stocks and shares ISA. Allowing up to £15,240 per annum investment.
- The tax advantages (and restrictions) are those which apply to ISA's.
- Additional life cover is required to cover the early death risk.
- ISA mortgages bear the same mortgage costs as other types.

"IT HAPPENED RIGHT AFTER I TOLD HIM THAT HIS LIFE POLICY MATURED..."

Mortgage Product Types

Variable Rate Mortgages

- Due to intense competition in the mortgage market very few new loans are taken out a pure variable rate basis.
- They are usually taken out if a substantial discount or cashback is available.
- Discounts allow a reduction in the lender's normal mortgage rate over a period of time.
- Nothing is owed at the end of the discount period, unlike the deferred interest mortgage of the past.

Base Rate Tracker Mortgage

- A variant of this mortgage is the Tracker loan. This loan tracks or follows a set interest rate such as the Bank of England base rate.

Fixed Rate Mortgages

- The rate of interest is fixed for an initial period of the loan.
- This is an advantage only if interest rates rise during the fixed rate period.
- A booking fee or arrangement fee is paid by the borrower (typically £800).
- This is to secure funds at a fixed rate of interest.
- After the fixed rate period, the loan reverts to a variable rate of interest.
- The borrower will have to pay redemption fees in the event of early redemption.
- These may be expressed as a number of months' interest.
- Their purpose is to dissuade borrowers from redeeming the loan if interest rates fall.
- The redemption fee period may be longer than the fixed rate period.

Capped Mortgages

- Similar to fixed rate mortgages except the rate of interest charged can fall below the capped rate, but not go above during the capped term.
- Older style versions also had a collar which was a lower rate which prevented the interest charged falling below this figure.
- Have you ever bounced a really bouncy rubber ball in between the floor and ceiling? Watch how it just goes up and down but never above the ceiling or below the floor. Same concept.

Cashback Mortgages

- A Cashback is a sum of money paid by the lender to the borrower on completion of a mortgage.
- The amount offered may be anything up to around £10,000. The factors which tend to lead to the larger cashbacks are:
    - Larger loans;
    - Smaller loan-to-value ratio.
- Clawback
    - In offering a cashback, the lender is effectively discounting the product against its income-generating potential over the whole term or a large proportion of it.
    - This is normally achieved by means of clawback
    - If a borrower redeems a cashback loan early (normally within the first five years, though periods vary), some or all of the cashback has to be returned by the borrower.

"AND IF YOU KEEP A MONTHLY MINIMUM BALANCE OF ONE THOUSAND, YOU ALSO ARE CONSIDERED TO BE ONE OF OUR BANK VICE-PRESIDENTS."

Flexible mortgages

- With the increasing popularity of the repayment mortgage and the need to satisfy consumer's demand vehicles for the next century ensured we had flexible mortgages.
- Their flexibility results from the following common features.
    - Interest calculated on a daily basis
    - Irregular payments facility – including overpayments, underpayments and payment holidays.
    - Additional borrowing facilities.
- Underpayments and payment holidays are restricted by the amount of overpayments the borrower has previously made. Additional borrowing facilities are agreed in advance up to a mortgage to value limit, often 75% to 80%.
- A key feature of flexible mortgages is their treatment of interest which is calculated on a daily basis. Borrowers therefore benefit immediately when overpayments are made.
- Competitive pressures have resulted in most lenders providing flexible facilities with no early redemption fees or charges.

Current Account or Off-Set Mortgage

- A variation of the Flexible mortgage is known as the Current Account Mortgage. The current account and mortgage account balances are offset against each other for the purposes of calculating interest on a mortgage.

Shared ownership mortgage

- This effectively combines rental with owner-occupation.
- The system is used extensively by housing associations, and enables people on lower incomes to progressively become owner-occupiers.
- A borrower purchases a certain "stake" (often 25%) in a property with the aid of a mortgage loan, whilst renting the remainder.
- The borrower has the option to buy further stakes later, thereby reducing the rental element. The process of increasing one's stake is known as "staircasing".

Deferred mortgages

- Relatively popular in the early 1990's when interest rates hit a peak of 15.4%. They were designed to assist the borrower to keep down costs in the early years, often by deferring capital repayments during a specified initial period.
- Unpaid interest was added to the outstanding capital balance.
- Attractive to those who want to maximise the loan and minimise the repayments in the early years.

"... AND IT KEEPS PEOPLE LIKE ME FROM BOTHERING YOU."

CAT Standard Mortgages

- CAT standard mortgages are mortgages that conform to minimum standards set out by the government.

	Variable rate	**Fixed or capped rate**
Charges	Interest calculated daily. Full credit for all payments when made. No separate charge for mortgage indemnity guarantee (MIG) Any other fees disclosed in cash up front. Borrowers pay no fees to brokers.	
	No arrangement fee. Interest rate no more than 2% above Bank of England base rate. When the base rate falls, interest rates must adjust within a calendar month. No redemption charges at any time.	Maximum booking fee is £150. The maximum redemption charge is 1% of the amount owed for each remaining year of fixed period, reducing monthly. No redemption charge after the fixed or capped rate period. No redemption charge if the borrower stays with the same mortgage lender when they move home.
Access	If there is a minimum amount that must be borrowed to get a CAT standard mortgage, it has to be £10,000 or less. Any customer may apply. The lender's normal lending criteria apply. Provided the lender is happy to lend on the new property, the borrower can continue with their CAT standard mortgage when they move home. If the borrower makes regular payments, they can choose which day of the month to pay. Early repayments can be made at any time.	
Terms	All advertising and paperwork must be straightforward, fair and clear. The borrower does not have to buy any other product to get a CAT standard mortgage. The lender must give at least six months' notice if they can no longer offer the mortgage on CAT standard terms. If the borrower is in arrears, they should pay interest only on the outstanding debt at the normal rate	

Buy To Let Mortgages

- Previously, buying a property to produce an income was considered by lenders to be a commercial undertaking.
- Therefore, mortgages on property intended to be let, have attracted higher interest rates than those available to owner-occupiers.
- Also, rental income was not usually allowed to be considered in the assessment of a borrower's ability to repay the mortgage.
- Things have now changed and many lenders consider that the private rented sector should be encouraged. Lack of choice between renting and buying is generally considered to be bad for the economy and may even have contributed to the booms and busts in the housing market over previous years.
- Generally Buy to Let mortgages are available for between five and 45 years and for up to 80% of the property value.
- Through the Buy-to-Let scheme, the rental income you get for the property can be taken into account.
- Generally, lenders will expect landlords to use a letting agent to manage the property and for the tenants contracts to be drawn up as Assured Shorthold Tenancies.
- Generally, your gross rents should be between 130% and 150% of your monthly mortgage repayment.
- Single rooms being let in the main residence of the borrower are usually of no concern to the lender. This is known as lodging.

FCA Regulation on Buy to Let Mortgages

- Previously Buy to Let mortgages were not regulated by the FCA since they fall outside of the 40% rule and are generally not lived in by family members.
- This has now changed with the FCA preferring to distinguish between:
    - Buy to Let mortgages arranged by a business and
    - Buy to Let mortgage arranged by an individual or consumer
- They're regulating the one arranged by a consumer but not the one organised by a business. The vast majority of professional landlords who use Buy to Let mortgages to build up their property portfolios, do so via a company of some sort to minimise taxation.
- The FCA recognises that some people inherit a buy to let mortgage with a let to buy, where their existing home is rented out on a temporary basis whilst they live elsewhere.
- These people need protection and the mortgage needs to be regulated. Providers of these will have to adhere to the MCOBs from now on.

Guarantee Mortgages

- A shift recently has allowed many lenders to offer Guarantee Mortgages.
- These simply add a guarantor to the mortgage deed which gives the lender someone else to call upon in the event of the borrower's inability to pay the monthly instalments.
- In addition, lenders can offer larger income multiples to enable the first time borrow to take a larger loan.
- Guarantors are normally relatives of the borrowers, you can have more than one, but their age mustn't be more than 65.

Releasing Equity for Elderly

Lifetime Mortgages

- The client(s) take an interest only loan secured on their home.
- No repayments are made and unpaid interest is rolled up and increases the outstanding debt.
- On death (or second death of a couple) the loan is repaid from the proceeds of the sale of the house.
- In the meantime, the owners agree to maintain and repair the property.
- Any increase in the value of the property between effecting the plan and death accrues to the estate of the deceased.

Home Income Plans

- Similarly a loan is secured on a home.
- They use the loan to buy a purchased life annuity providing income for life (or until the second death in the case of couples).
- Part of the annuity income is used to pay the interest on the loan.
- The remainder forms spendable income for the client.
- On death (or second death of a couple) the loan is repaid from the proceeds of the sale of the house.
- Tax relief is still available but only from plans arranged before 1999.

Home Reversion Schemes

- The company takes over ownership of the property, but permits the former owner to remain in occupation until death, or second death of a couple (who in turn agree to keep the property in good repair).
- In exchange the company pays a lump sum (less than the current value of the property) or an income for life.
- In this case, any increase in the value of the property accrues to the company.
- Since April 2007, these have become regulated by the FCA.

Further Borrowing

Further advance

- A further advance from the existing lender.
- Usually over the remaining term of the existing loan.
- New plus existing may be restricted to, say, 85% of the property value.
- Some lenders may offer further advances only for improvements to the property.

Remortgage

- New lender takes over the existing borrowing and lends an additional amount as well.

Secured second mortgages

- People who require to release equity for a purpose not related to the property (e.g. buy a car or to finance a business deal) may choose a second mortgage.
- This is an additional loan from a different lender, sitting on top of the original mortgage and secured by a second charge on the property.
- Interest rates are generally higher than the other methods, as the lender's security is less.
- If the borrower defaults on this loan, the property can be sold – the main mortgage would be redeemed first out of the sale proceeds, then the second mortgage.

Unsecured loans

- Involve no security just a personal covenant or promise to pay.
- Therefore higher risk for the lender who charge a higher rate of interest.
- Known as personal loans

Pension Products

Occupational Pensions

- Available to those in employment.
- A final salary scheme is based on the employee's salary on retirement. The longer they belong to the scheme – the greater the fraction of their final salary will be paid.
- A money purchase scheme involves contributions from the employer and the employee (your boss and you). The more money that is contributed, the bigger the pension.

Nest – National Employment Savings Trust

- The government has introduced new legislation which means all companies will have to automatically enrol their eligible workers into a contributory pension plan.
- This requirement will be gradually phased in, beginning with the largest employers in 2012.
- NEST (National Employment Savings Trust) is a pension scheme which has been designed to meet the employer's responsibilities. It has been designed to be a low cost option, simple and available to all employers, irrelevant of their size.
- NEST has been designed to provide employees with access to a pension plan. However, there may be other pension schemes which are more suitable to an individual's circumstances.
- For high earners and others requiring more diverse investment options, then NEST may not be suitable.
- From October 2012, employers will be required to auto enrol eligible employees into the NEST Pension Scheme (unless you already have a company pension scheme which meets all the qualifying criteria or you have already set up a qualifying scheme).
- NESTs have low fees, a default investment fund, limited choice of investment funds
- A limit of £4,700 a year contribution

Private Arrangements

- Private arrangements include:
    - Additional Voluntary Contributions (AVCs).
    - Free Standing Additional Voluntary Contributions (FSAVCs).
    - Personal Pensions or Stakeholder Pensions.
    - Pension Term Assurance.

Additional voluntary contributions

- These are paid by employees who belong to an occupational pension scheme and are run by the same people who run the main scheme.
- They provide extra income to the employee in return for higher monthly contributions.
- Full tax relief is available at source.

Free standing additional voluntary contributions

- FSAVCs are provided by life offices and other pension providers, rather than by occupational schemes.
- It is expected that FSAVCs will be phased out as employees are now able to contribute to stakeholder pensions which are much cheaper.

Personal Pensions

- Where you read personal pensions you should be thinking stakeholder pensions – they are broadly the same.
- They are available to any UK Resident under the age of 75. This is employed people, self-employed, unemployed, children – anyone.
- The most someone can contribute to their stakeholder pension is 100% of their annual income or £40,000 whichever is the higher figure.
- However, you can carry forward unused allowances for up to 3 years.
- There is also a life allowance restricting the fund to £1.25 million.
- The pension fund will accumulate free of income tax and capital gains tax on investment gains.
- Contributions are paid net of basic tax for everyone, whether they pay tax or not. Higher rate tax payers recover the balance through their self-assessment.
- Other Stakeholder features:
  - An annual charge of no more than 1.5% of the fund for the first ten years, then 1% thereafter.
  - The minimum contribution to a stakeholder pension cannot be more than £20 and contributions can be weekly, monthly or at other intervals, or can be single, one-off, contributions.
  - They have the ability to stop and start contributions without penalty.
- You can take your benefits from age 55. You can take up to 25% of your pension fund as a tax-free lump sum.
- The rest of the fund is used to buy an income (an annuity) which will be taxable. You can use an Open Market Option to buy the best annuity on the market.
- Alternatively you can simply draw money from your fund until you are ready to buy your annuity. This is known as drawdown. There is now no upper age here, so you can drawdown indefinitely.
- The amount of the drawdown is arranged by the Government Actuarial Department (GAD) who determine the GAD limit. You can drawdown between 0% and 150% of the GAD limit.

Personal Pensions – Radical Changes

- It's all change for the pension's world and these changes affect your CeMAP exams quite a bit. CeMAP 1 is all about the pension products and CeMAP 2 focusses your mind on Pension Linked Mortgages.

Tax Relief

- Tax relief is going to be slowly taken away but is still available this year, so the Personal Pension is still an excellent way to save for your retirement years, with full tax relief available, a very tax efficient fund growth and tax benefits when you take your money, after age 55.

Contributions

- Contributions to the Personal Pension are capped at £40,000 or your income whichever comes first. This prevents people putting too much in.
- If you're not earning or can't prove income, the limit is £3,600 each year. You can also bring forward the previous 2 years' unused allowances if you have a large sum to invest.

Fund Growth

- Growth of the fund is also capped. Called the Lifetime Allowance, you can't build up a pension pot of more than £1,000,000 from April 2016. Although this seems like a huge sum is does have an influence of the money at retirement.

Death

- If you die before age 75 and you haven't taken your pension, the fund is returned to your beneficiaries free of tax.
- Dying after age 75, will incur a tax charge on the remaining pension pot as it transfers to your beneficiaries.

Options at age 55

- Tax Free Lump Sum
    - Up to 25% of the whole fund, can be taken as a tax free lump sum. Traditionally, this was the amount that was geared towards repaying an interest only mortgage.
- Uncrystallised funds pension lump sum
    - This means taking the whole pension pot as a lump sum. How tempting is this, but you'll need to bear in mind that the whole sum (excluding the 25% tax free part) is liable to your marginal rate of tax. Remember it's the whole sum, so this would very easily push a non-taxpayer into high rate tax.
    - Pension Linked Mortgages can now gear themselves to the entire pot, not just the 25% tax free element, although the tax charge is quite hefty. I can see a few people repaying their mortgages in this manner.
    - You can take smaller lump sums when you want to, after age 55. These would also be taxable but with some careful planning, you might minimise this.
- Flexi Access Drawdown (FAD)
    - We live in a world with too many acronyms – I mean FAD!
    - Here you can take your 25% tax free lump sum, and then draw off an income from the actual pension pot. The income is taxable but the pension pot remains invested and you can still contribute if you wish (up to £10,000 per year).

3 The Financial Planning Process

Financial Life Cycle

- School-age
    - Under age 18. Normally dependent on parents, who take responsibility for financial planning, e.g. education costs, first car, wedding.
- Teens and students.
    - Little opportunity for saving! May have to consider how to repay student loans.
- Post education.
    - First experience of regular income. Probably few responsibilities. Save towards emergency fund and/or house deposit? Insure against inability to work due to sickness/accident.
- Newly married.
    - Mortgage costs: typically one-third of net income. Need to protect income of both partners. Many other costs of setting up home.
- Parent.
    - Loss of one income. Cost of raising children (£1,500 per child p.a.?). Need to insure lives of both parents. Planning for school or university fees.

- Mature households.
  - Family grown and left home. May be surplus funds available after outgoings met. Possibility of receiving inheritances. Pension planning starts to become very important - and costly, especially as a result of changing jobs often. Mortgage may be paid off.
- Retirement.
  - When to retire (can you afford to?). What level of income required, what standard of living? Need to convert capital into lifetime income.

Gathering information

- Complete fact-find; view other financial documents; determine client's preferences; use pertinent questioning.
- Identify customer's needs and objectives.
- Agree customer's needs and objectives.
- Agree order of priority for meeting needs and objectives.
- Match solutions to needs and objectives.
- Present recommended solutions.
- Agree solutions with customer.
- Complete documentation.
- Client-specific illustration; application form; suitability letter.
- Maintain appropriate records.
- For compliance auditing; to assist in the event of a complaint or dispute.
- Review needs and objectives with customer at agreed intervals.
- Good after-sales service. Opportunities for additional business or introductions.

Contents of a Factfind

- Personal details.
    - Name, address, telephone number.
    - Date and place of birth, also details of domicile/residence if not UK.
    - Marital status (or long-term relationship).
    - State of health.
- Family details: (indicate what benefits might be required).
    - Spouse/partner.
    - Children.
    - Other dependants.
- Employment details.
    - Occupation and employer.
    - Basic income, other income, benefits in kind.
    - Pension, life cover, sickness schemes, etc.
- Assets.
    - Main residence and any other property.
    - Personal belongings.
    - Savings and investments.
- Liabilities.
    - Mortgage.
    - Other loans.
    - Details of which are covered by life/sickness/redundancy insurance.
- Life assurance and regular savings.
- Pension arrangements.
- Income and expenditure.
    - A detailed summary of monthly income and outgoings.
- Attitude and objectives.

4 Financial Services Legal Concepts

Personal Representatives

- These are people who carry out the distribution of an estate.
- The procedure depends on whether a Will has been made or not.
- If a Will has been made, the Personal Representatives make an application to the Probate Office. They are given a Grant of Probate which details the Executor who has power to distribute the estate according to the terms of the Will
- Where there is no Will, the Personal Representative makes the same application to the Probate Office but is issued with Letters of Administration. The Administrator must then distribute the estate according to the Law of Intestacy.

Wills

- A will is a declaration made by a person (the testator) to state what they wish to happen to their property after their death.
- Normally a will relates mainly to the disposal of assets but it may also give instructions as to burial.
- It should appoint executor(s) whose task will be to carry out the deceased's wishes.
- It must be in writing, typed or printed (not verbal).
- It must be signed by testator (or by someone else in his presence and on his instructions if, for instance, he cannot write).
- The testator's signature must be witnessed by two witnesses who must not be beneficiaries under the will.
- A will becomes invalid if :
    - It is destroyed by the testator with intent to revoke it.
    - The testator makes a later will.
    - The testator marries or remarries.
- Deed of Variation
    - Enables change of a Will up to 2 years after the death of the testator (holder of the will)
    - Normally used to avoid an excessive IHT from a badly worded will
    - All parties must be agreeable to the changes

Intestacy

- Intestacy results when no will has been made
- Disadvantages of intestacy include :
  - Some or all of the estate may not go to those whom the deceased would have wished to benefit.
  - It may take longer for the estate to be distributed.
  - There may be additional Inheritance Tax liability due to less of the estate going to the spouse.

Intestacy Rules for England and Wales

- Revised by Inheritance and Trustees Powers Act 2014

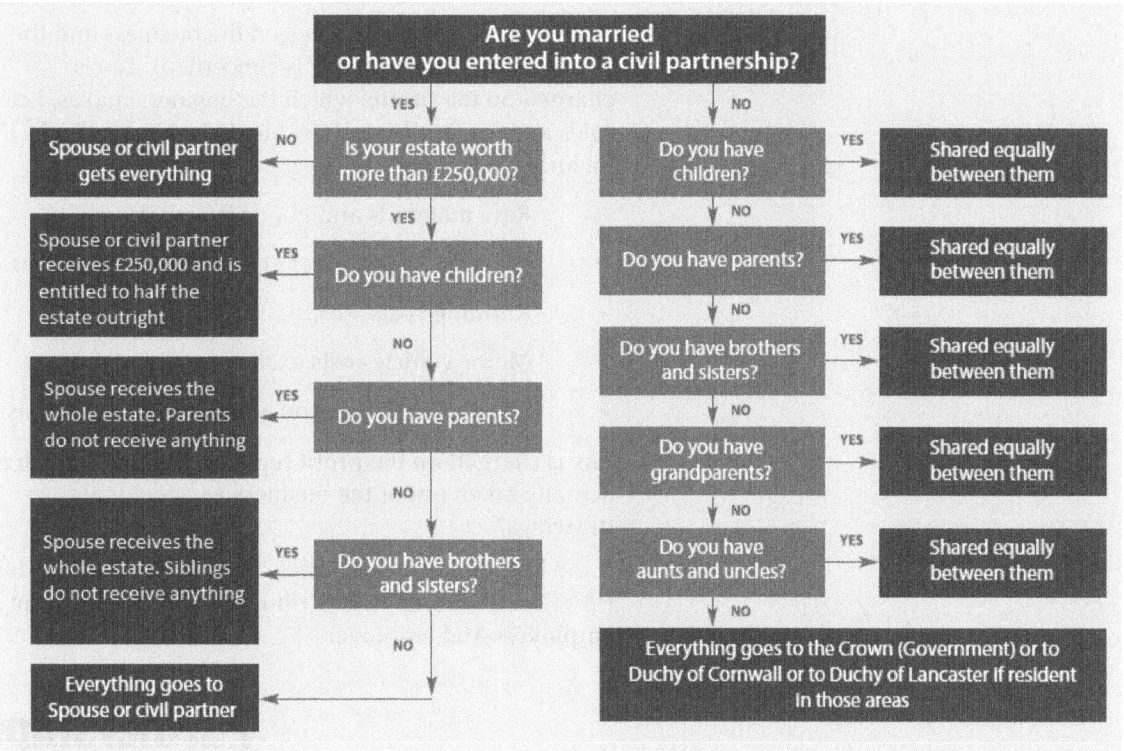

Sole Traders, Partnerships and Charities

Sole trader

- Self-employed individual running own business.
- No distinction is made between the business and the owner as far as income tax is concerned. Tax is charged on the profits which the business makes, i.e. sales and/or fees less allowable deductions, which include:
    - Raw materials and goods for resale.
    - Wages, NI, and other staff costs of employees.
    - Running costs: electricity, phone etc.
    - Motor vehicle costs excluding private use.
    - Capital allowances on a "writing down" basis.
- Tax is charged on the profit regardless of how much is actually taken out of the business as "personal drawings".
- If the business has employees, they will pay tax under PAYE, and Class 1 NI contributions will be due from employees and employer.

Partnerships

- Partners are effectively self-employed and each pays tax on their own share of the partnership profits. Each partner's NI contributions are based on this amount.
- Under self-assessment, partners are individually liable for the income tax on their share of the profits.

Financial Services Legal Concepts

Limited Liability Partnerships

- The Limited Liability Partnerships Act 2000 creates a new type of business entity, the Limited Liability Partnership ("LLP"). The LLP offers limited liability to its members but is tax transparent and offers flexibility in terms of its internal organisation.

- LLPs have been available for use since 6 April, 2001.

- An LLP is a separate legal entity from its members. Therefore, it may enter into contracts and deeds, sue and be sued.

- An LLP has unlimited capacity. There is no memorandum of association, as there is with limited companies, restricting what the LLP may do.

- Members of an LLP have limited liability up to the amount of their capital in the LLP.

- Provided an LLP carries on a trade or a profession and is not simply an investment vehicle it is tax transparent – that is the LLP itself is not taxed on its income or capital gains at all. Instead the members are taxed on their shares of the LLPs profits and gains, just as partners in a partnership are currently taxed.

Charities

- Charities are exempt from income tax, corporation tax and capital gains tax. They must pay VAT and cannot reclaim it.

Contract law

- There are a number of requirements for valid contract. These include:
    - There must be offer and acceptance and consideration.
- The contract must have a legal purpose:
- The terms of the contract must be certain, complete, and free from doubt.
- For instance, if the subject matter of the contract did not exist, the contract would be void.
- If one party fails to keep to the terms of the contract, the other party has a number of possible remedies:
    - He could simply choose not to perform his part of the contract, although this is often not possible (e.g. the payment has already been made).
    - He could seek damages, i.e. financial compensation for his loss.
    - He could obtain an injunction, which is a court order compelling the other party to do something - or refrain from doing it.
- Under most contracts the principle of "caveat emptor" - let the buyer beware - applies. This means that there is no duty of disclosure between parties to the contract.
- However, there are exceptions - including life assurance contracts, to which a different principle applies. This is the principle of *utmost good faith*, which means that all material facts must be disclosed.
- A life assurance applicant must therefore disclose all those facts which a prudent underwriter might need to know in order to decide the terms on which a policy could be issued.

Trusts

- A trust (sometimes called a settlement), is a legally enforceable obligation placed by one person, the settler, on persons called trustees, who must look after and deal with certain specified money or goods (the trust property) for the benefit of the beneficiaries, in accordance with the terms of the trust deed.
- A trust therefore enables property to be held for the benefit of others without giving them control over it.
- The settlor is the original owner of the property to be placed in trust, and:
  - ➢ Chooses the type of trust.
  - ➢ Appoints trustees (the settlor can be a trustee).
  - ➢ Nominates the beneficiaries and decides how they are to benefit.
- Trust property can be more or less anything, including life assurance policies.
- Trustees are the legal owners of the trust property. They must:
  - ➢ Be over 18, and of sound mind.
  - ➢ Deal with the trust property in accordance with the trust document .act in the best interests of the beneficiaries.
  - ➢ Act impartially where the interests of beneficiaries may conflict.
- Beneficiaries can be named as individuals or as classes (e.g. "my children").
- The Trustee Act 2000 requires that trustees are aware of the need for diversification in investments, the need for professional guidance and to keep investments under review.

Consumer Insurance Act 2012

- The Consumer Insurance (Disclosure and Representations) Act 2012 came into force on 6th April 2013. It removes the duty on consumers to disclose any facts that a prudent underwriter would consider material and replaces this with a duty to take reasonable care not to make a misrepresentation.

- The Act does not currently apply to commercial insurance but will nevertheless have a significant impact on insurance distribution. The Insurance Act of 2015 takes care of the commercial insurance side.

- The Act will abolish the consumer's duty to volunteer facts that an underwriter might consider material - instead, consumers must take reasonable care to answer questions that are asked by insurers.

- The onus now sits squarely with the insurer to ask you the questions that they want to know information about. Instead of a duty to volunteer material facts, now the law requires you to answer the questions that are put to you fully and accurately. You need to "take reasonable care", and one of the factors that will be taken into account is whether the questions asked by the insurer were clear and specific.

- So, forms may get a little longer because the onus is on the insurer to ask you the right questions. Insurers should no longer be making reference to a "duty of disclosure".

Financial Services Legal Concepts

Agency Law

- An agent is a person who acts on behalf of someone else (who is called the principal).
- A tied agent or company representative acts as the agent of the product provider, whereas an independent financial adviser (IFA) is acting as the agent of the client.
- In law, the actions of the agent are treated as the actions of (and are therefore binding on) the principal.
- It is therefore essential that the extent of the authority, given to the agent to act on the principal's behalf, should be made clear.

Apparent Authority

- If an agent acts outside that stated authority, but it can be shown that the principal has given the impression that he has authorised what the agent has done, then it will be binding on the principal.
- On the other hand, in order to safeguard the position of the third party, if it can be shown that the agent has exceeded his authority, then the agent may become liable.

Ratification

- The principal could, of course, choose to agree after the event to ratify what the agent has done.

Ownership of Property

Legal Types of property

- *Realty* is property that cannot be destroyed and the best example is land (unless a nuclear device goes off).
- Property is "real" if a court will restore it to a dispossessed owner, rather than merely provide compensation.
- The Americans use the term Real Estate for land and buildings. In practical terms, the main property is also realty.
- In the photo, the land behind the gate would be realty
- *Personalty* is all other property.
- Theoretically, leased property is *personalty*, but it is generally regarded for practical purposes as real estate.

Financial Services Legal Concepts

Joint tenancy

- Two or more people own an asset jointly and severally.
- On death, the whole asset belongs to the survivor, and none of it to the beneficiaries of the estate of the deceased.
- Typically arranged for property ownership by married couples.

Tenancy in common

- An asset is held on a split basis, usually - but not necessarily - in equal shares.
- On the death of one party, their share of an asset held on this basis passes to their estate, not to the surviving person(s).
- Tenants in Common ownership tends to be for unmarried couples such as brothers buying together.

Trustees

- Have the responsibility of dealing with trust property, in accordance with the terms of a trust deed, in the interests of the beneficiaries.

Power of Attorney

- People who legally act on behalf of others.
- Person who makes the Power is the donor.
- Cannot be a minor or mentally incapacitated
- Lasting Power of Attorney is established when the person is of sound mind but comes into force when they become mentally incapacitated.
- It's a bit like buying breakdown cover for your car which you only activate when the car breaks down.

Insolvency and Bankruptcy

Bankruptcy

- A person's liabilities exceed his assets;
  - A person cannot meet his financial obligations within a reasonable period of their falling due.
- The order usually remains in force for 1 year under the Enterprise Act 2002.
- During this time;
  - The person is an undischarged bankrupt.
  - He cannot borrow more than nominal amounts.
- After that time;
  - He can borrow, if a lender is prepared to lend.
  - Earlier bankruptcy must be declared.

Individual voluntary arrangements (IVAs)

- An IVA is an alternative to bankruptcy.
- The debtor arranges with creditors to reschedule outstanding debts over a certain period.
- Creditors who represent 75% of the debts must agree to the arrangement.
- Persons subject to IVAs are a poor credit risk and would find it difficult to borrow during the IVA period.

Company Voluntary Arrangements

- Known as a CVA.
- Route frequently taken by directors who feel their company has a viable future.
- Directors keep control and trade as normal.
- Agreements made with creditors.
- All or part of the company's debts repaid over a period of time from the trading profits.

Financial Services Legal Concepts

Debt Relief Orders

- Brought in as a result of legislation, DROs allow people in debt to receive years grace and then for the loans to be wiped out. These people will have their credit record tarnished for many years to come.
- People need to be struggling with debt, have limited disposable income and no assets
- After a year of the lenders not being able to enforce payments, so long as they have kept to the conditions, the debts are written off.
- The Insolvency Service and approved advisers can arrange DROs
- Conditions to apply are:
    - Domiciled in England and Wales
    - Owe £15,000 maximum
    - Have assets of no more than £300
    - Have a disposable income of no more than £50
    - Not have applied for bankruptcy or a DRO in the previous 6 years

Behaving badly is not an option this time

Richard Evans and **Emma Wall** explain the alternatives to bankruptcy when facing ruin

He is best known as the star of the comedy television show *Men Behaving Badly*, but Neil Morrissey has joined the growing number of people who have entered into an individual voluntary arrangement, after losing £2.5m in a collapsed property scheme.

The actor, who lives in Crouch End, north London, said he had lost £2.5m after investing in hotels and pubs. He said he would not file for bankruptcy and intended to pay his creditors in full.

"Bankruptcy's the easy way out," he said. "I decided no, I'd step up to the plate, try to do the right thing and get everyone their money back."

Morrissey has instead entered into an individual voluntary arrangement (IVA), which means that all his earnings, minus his living

> **Bankruptcy is the easy way out. I decided I'd try to do the right thing**

costs, will go to his creditors for more than three years.

He said: "People advise you to take the easy route [bankruptcy] – it'll only last a year and you'll be back up and running. But I just thought there are too many good people who've lost their money on these deals, and I wanted to repay them as much as I possibly could.

"I feel morally obliged. Afterwards I'll feel better about myself. Now I'm working very, very hard every second out there to earn another penny. I don't sit around and get depressed about things. It's not my character."

Morrissey, who provided some of the voices in the children's television show *Bob the Builder*, set up a property company five years ago. It bought pubs and hotels around the country, including Brown's Hotel in Laugharne, where the Welsh poet Dylan Thomas was a regular.

The company overstretched itself and collapsed, forcing Morrissey's business partner into bankruptcy.

Mr Morrissey is just one of 60,000 people to have been declared insolvent this year. This is the highest level since records began in 1960 and 27pc more than during the same quarter of 2008, according to the Insolvency Service.

But insolvency practitioners warned that as many as 150,000 people could be declared insolvent during 2009 as the credit crisis prevents people from restructuring their debts, while rising unemployment makes it harder for people to keep up with borrowings.

People who run into financial difficulty have two main options. They can declare themselves bankrupt or, as in the case of Morrissey, enter into an IVA. People with less than £15,000 of debts can also take out a debt relief order (DRO), which was introduced only in April and so far accounts for a small percentage of insolvencies.

But what is the difference between an IVA and a bankruptcy order? And what is the best option for people in financial difficulty?

The main differences are that assets are handled differently, the home is treated differently and the time periods for each procedure are different. Also, employment status has to be considered before choosing.

IVAs were introduced to provide individuals with an alternative to bankruptcy. The types of debts dealt with by IVAs can include personal loans and credit card balances. An IVA is a legally binding contract between a debtor and their creditors. It allows an individual to settle a debt within a reasonable and fixed period of time, usually five years, according to a contract.

The debtor will make monthly payments, typically a minimum of £200, to the insolvency practitioner based on what it is agreed the debtor can afford. Once the final payment is made, any remaining debt is legally written off.

Bob Kingdon, from debt collection agency 1st Credit, said: "The past few years have seen a surge in the number of insolvency practitioners offering IVAs, and while they may be the best solution for some, we would advise people to first seek free debt advice from organisations such as the Consumer Credit Counselling Service, Christians Against Poverty or Citizens Advice."

A bankruptcy order may be obtained by any creditor for debts of £750 or more. Alternatively, a debtor can bankrupt himself by filling in the relevant forms at a county court. The debtor's assets are then sold and the money is distributed – after the insolvency practitioner's costs – to creditors. Assets that are exempt include tools of trade, pensions, ordinary household contents and possessions, including a car.

In most cases, bankruptcy ends after one year or less, when the slate is wiped clean. One of the biggest setbacks with bankruptcy is that you may lose your assets – including your house. The IVA process is different; you may have to remortgage, but you should be able to keep the property.

Bankruptcy is also a public matter – legally, there are some parties that must be informed, such as your bank. It will also be published in newspapers, so you will not be able to control who finds out. An IVA is a more private option. While your IVA will be published on the Insolvency Service website, it will not be published in any newspapers.

Going bankrupt can take the pressure of creditors away from you. You are allowed to keep certain things, such as household goods, and a reasonable amount to live on. When the bankruptcy order

5 The Regulation of Financial Services

Current Regulation

- The Government has now given The Bank of England wide powers to regulate the financial services industry.

- The Financial Policy Committee (FPC) has been created within the Bank of England to monitor the economy and keeping a "big picture" overview.

- The Prudential Regulation Authority (PRA) reports to the Bank of England and regulates banks and other large institutions – those that offer a systemic risk.

- The Financial Conduct Authority (FCA) reports direct to the Treasury and is responsible for protecting consumers and authorising firms

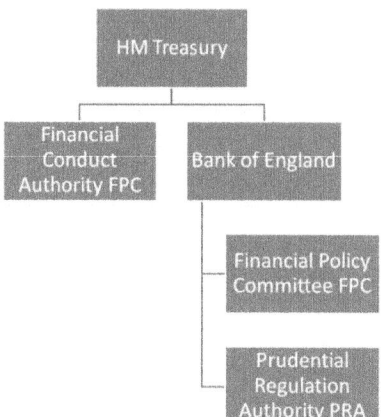

Main Legislation

Financial Services and Markets Act 2000

- The aim of this Act was to bring together regulation of the entire financial services market, which previously, was rather fragmented.

- The Financial Services Authority (FSA) was put in place as the single regulatory body.

- The Financial Ombudsman Service (FOS) was set up dealing with complaints from across the entire sector.

- The Financial Services Compensation Scheme (FSCS) was set up to provide compensation.

- Over time, the vast majority of products became regulated. Known as regulated activities, these were:
  - Deposits
  - Stocks and Shares
  - Gilts
  - Futures
  - Unit Trusts and OEICs

- Over the next 10 years more were added:
  - Funeral plans from 2002
  - Mortgages from 2004
  - General insurance from 2005
  - SIPPS and home reversion plans from 2007
  - Travel insurance from 2009
  - Sale and rent back schemes from 2009

Financial Services Act 2012

- Commencing in April 2012 and significantly reforming the system set up by the FSMA.
- Gives the Chancellor of the Exchequer powers to direct the Bank of England.
- Gives the Bank of England macro responsibility to oversee the financial system via the FPC and to act upon systemic risks i.e. those that can endanger the whole financial services sector such as the banking crisis of 2008.
- Dismantled the FSA and created the FCA to supervise all firms.

Markets in Financial Instruments Directive (MiFID)

- Came into effect 2007.
- Sets out detailed requirements for the organisation and conduct of business of investment firms such as investment banks, insurance brokers, futures and options firms.
- Most IFA firms deal with UK customers only so fall out of the remit of MiFID
- Provides single set of rules making it easier to transact business across the EU.
- Gives investment firms their Capital Requirements Directive

MiFID II

- Revision to improve the functioning of financial markets in light of the financial crisis and to strengthen investor protection.
- Changes to take effect from January 2017. Components:
    - Commodity Derivatives
    - Transparency
    - High frequency trading
    - Market structure
    - Organisational requirements
    - Trade reporting
    - Conduct of business rules
    - Transaction reporting

CeMAP 1 Revision Guide

Regulatory Aims and Objectives

FCA Regulatory Principles

- 6 Principles:
  - Efficiency and economy so it uses its resources correctly
  - Proportionality to ensure a cost benefit analysis is used when proposing regulatory changes to avoid a low return on investment.
  - Responsibility of consumers to ensure consumers take responsibility for their own decisions
  - Senior Management to be responsible for regulation within their business.
  - Openness and disclosure so that all information is published openly and consumers are educated, if they desire.
  - Transparency

FCA – 3 Objectives

- Consumer protection
- Integrity
  - Soundness and integrity of firms
  - Combating market abuse
  - Addressing financial crime within the sector
- Competition
  - Seeks to promote competition within the sector to the advantage of consumers
  - To encourage innovation, price competitiveness, better products and services

The Regulation of Financial Services

PRA Objectives

- The PRA authorises banks, building societies, credit unions, insurers and major investment firms.

- It's main objective is to promote the safety and soundness of these firms to protect the consumer ultimately.

- With a stable financial services system creates a constantly performing economy.

- Often called "Twin Peaks", the PRA will work closely with the FCA.

FCA Scope and Powers

Authorisation

- Smaller firms will be authorised by the FCA and must apply for direct authorisation unless they remain exempt.
- Known as Part 4A permissions.

FCA Powers

- To authorise firms and grant permitted activities
- To approve individuals to carry out controlled functions
- To authorise unit trusts
- To maintain a public record of authorised persons
- To supervise firms over their conduct of business, client money, financial promotions.
- To fight money laundering
- To impose penalties for abuse
- To carry out investigations and take disciplinary action
- To prosecute for insider trading as a result of inside dealing, misuse of information, manipulating transactions and misleading behaviour
- To levy penalties on businesses in breach of Money Laundering Regulations

FCA Principles

Integrity

- A firm must conduct its business with integrity.

Skill, care and diligence

- A firm must conduct its business with due skill, care, and diligence.

Management and control

- A firm must take reasonable care to organise and control its affairs responsibly and effectively, with adequate risk management systems.

Financial prudence

- A firm must maintain adequate financial resources.

Market conduct

- A firm must observe proper standards of market conduct.

Customers interests

- A firm must pay due regard to the interests of its customers and treat them fairly.

Communications with clients

- A firm must pay due regard to the information needs of its clients, and communicate information to them in a way which is clear, fair, and not misleading.

Conflicts of interest

- A firm must manage conflicts of interest fairly, both between itself and its customers, and between one customer and another client.

Customers – relationships of trust

- A firm must take reasonable care to ensure the suitability of its advice and discretionary decisions for any customer who is entitled to rely on its judgement.

Clients assets

- A firm must arrange adequate protection for clients assets when it is responsible for them.

Relations with regulators

- A firm must deal with its regulators in an open and cooperative way, and must disclose to the FCA appropriately anything relating to the firm of which the FCA would reasonably expect notice.

FCA Principles for Approved Persons

- Statement of Principle 1
  - An approved person must act with integrity in carrying out his controlled function.

- Statement of Principle 2
  - An approved person must act with due skill, care and diligence in carrying out his controlled function.

- Statement of Principle 3
  - An approved person must observe proper standards of market conduct in carrying out his controlled function.

- Statement of Principle 4
  - An approved person must deal with the FCA and with other regulators in an open and cooperative way and just disclose appropriately any information of which the FCA would reasonably expect notice.

- Statement of Principle 5
  - An approved person performing a significant influence function must take reasonable steps to ensure that the business of the firm for which he is responsible in his controlled function is organised so that it can be controlled effectively.

- Statement of Principle 6
  - An approved person performing a significant influence function must exercise due skill, care and diligence in managing the business of the firm for which he is responsible in his controlled function.

- Statement of Principle 7
  - An approved person must take reasonable steps to ensure that the business of the firm for which he is responsible in his controlled function complies with the relevant requirements. Items 5 to 7 apply to senior management only.

Prudential Regulation

Talk to Prudence?

- Nothing to do with the woman from the Pru. Prudential regulation imposes standards that require firms to control risks and hold adequate capital, with the goal of protecting the markets from the sort of meltdown that is currently under way.

- Prudential rules contained in FCA Handbook

Capital Adequacy

- The point behind capital adequacy is that if you're going to take people's money on deposit and make money from this money via lending or other investments, you need to have some of your own money, or capital, just in case things go wrong.

Liquidity

- Banks need access to liquid funds to meet their outgoings.

- Liquid funds are those that can be quickly turned into cash.

- Managing your liquidity risk is the process of predicting how much liquid funds are needed to meet your expected outgoings and then matching this prediction with the required liquidity.

- Banks commitments include depositors, pre-arranged overdrafts and loans and credit cards limits.

The Regulation of Financial Services

Credit Crunch

- September 2007 witnessed the first run on a British bank in hundreds of years.

- The Northern Rock had a run on their assets and without the required liquidity, went cap in hand to the Bank of England for a loan as the lender of the last resort.

- Throughout the decade there has been a shift from retail funding to wholesale funding and as a result much of the lender's mortgage assets were secured not by depositors' money, but by a complex array of wholesale loans, syndicated loans and securitised assets.

- The credit crunch caused these assets to be extremely non-liquid. As the wholesale market dried up for future funding, the banks found themselves in disastrous liquid positions which were quickly remedied by Gordon Brown's initiative to pump billions of pounds into the UK banking system, nationalising some of the banks along the way.

" A DOLLAR FOR THE LOTTERY, SIR? "

Basel Committee

- Basel Committee on Banking Supervision sets global standards for prudential regulation
- Basel I
  - Published minimum set of capital requirements for banks
- Basel II
  - Details capital requirements for banks
  - More effective supervisory tools
  - Set of disclosure requirements.
- Basel III
  - Phased in up to March 2019
  - Banks required to have at least 7% of their own money compared to loans outstanding.
  - Different loans are weighted according to their risk i.e. unsecured lending and mortgage lending.
- Capital Requirements Directives are how the European Union have implemented the Basel accords.

Solvency II Directive

- Legislation for insurance companies which goes live in January 2016
- Directive that stipulates capital adequacy of insurers
- Main aims:
  - Reduce risk of not being able to cover claims and protects customers
  - Regular disclosure to the regulators
  - Promotes confidence in the sector
- Solvency margin for insurance based investment provider e.g. endowment policies is 4%

The Regulation of Financial Services

FCA/PRA Prudential Standards

- Already summarised in FSA Principle – a firm must maintain adequate financial resources.
- GENPRU
  - Requirements for all firms to hold capital
  - The amounts of capital to hold
  - Firms which cross the sectors e.g. Bancassurer
- BIPRU
  - Minimum capital requirements for banks, building societies, insurers
- IFPRU
  - Gives investment firms their Capital Requirements.
  - When dealing with private clients they must have €125,000 capital.
  - When dealing with other businesses, they must have €730,000 capital
- MIPRU
  - Capital requirements and professional indemnity requirement s for mortgage and home finance firms.

"WE'RE LIVING IN A WORLD OF LOWERED EXPECTATIONS."

2015/2016

Treating Customers Fairly

- Treating Customers Fairly or TCF, which kind of sounds like something you gurgle in your throat, is making a massive impact to financial services firms.

- In the past, establishing rules didn't get to the core of changing attitudes in financial services companies.

- So the FCA are now focussing their attention on making sure firms treat all their customers fairly.

What is TCF?

- The FCA refuses to define "fair" allowing firms to make that definition

- TCF must be evident throughout the life cycle of a product.

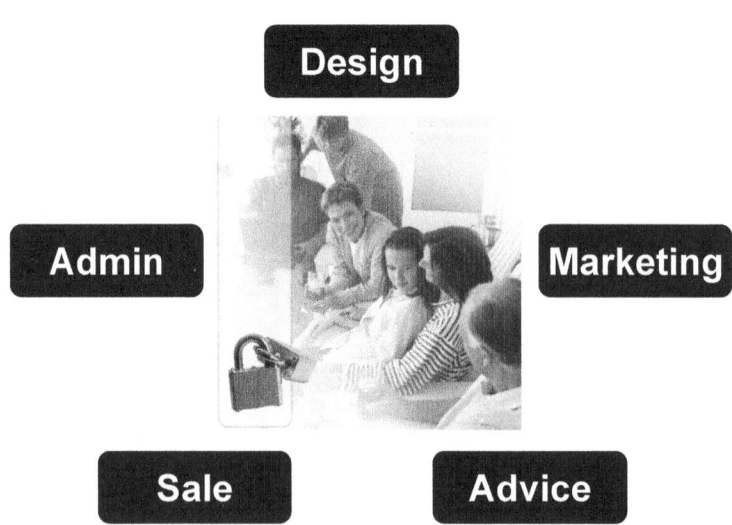

- Senior Management are responsible for TCF in their firms.

The Six TCF Deliverables

1. Consumers must know that they are being treated well.

2. Products are designed to meet the needs of properly identified customer groups.

3. Customers get clear information all the time.

4. Customer's situation has been assessed before advice is given.

5. Products perform as customers expect them to make it easy for customers to switch companies and to make claims.

6. No unreasonable barrier to switching

"BEFORE HE MAKES HIS DECISION ABOUT YOUR REPRIEVE, THE GOVERNOR WOULD LIKE TO KNOW IF YOU VOTED FOR HIM IN THE LAST ELECTION."

Systems and Controls

Approved persons

- Individuals who have received approval to carry out controlled functions are known as "approved persons".
- There are two kinds of approved persons:
  - Those who carry out senior or supervisory functions and are said to exercise "significant influence" over the firm.
  - Those who act in a customer-related field, typically in the role of adviser.

Controlled Functions

- Governing functions such as Director, Chief Executive
- Required functions such as compliance, money laundering
- System and control functions
- Significant management functions
- Customer dealing functions

Fit and Proper Test

- A rigid test carried out on all approved persons.
- Looks at:
  - Honesty, integrity and reputation
  - Competence and capability
  - Financial soundness

The Senior Manager's Regime

- The Senior Managers Regime (SMR) is on its way for senior bank executives and relevant non-executives.

- The FCA has seen that fining firms alone is not enough, and consequently those at the top will be held more accountable for any failings.

- It's being introduced in March 2016 for:
    - Banks, building societies and credit unions
    - PRA Designated Investment firms

Certification regime

- An individual who does not hold an SMF (Senior Manager Function), will be subject to the Certification Regime if they pose a risk of significant harm to a firm or its customers. The firm will need to satisfy itself on an ongoing basis, as to the fitness and propriety of those under the Certification Regime.

Conduct rules

- This is a new set of rules that set out the standards of behaviour for bank employees. There one set for all relevant individuals, and an additional set for senior managers. Both groups will need to be trained on the rules so that they understand them in the context of their roles.

Responsibilities map

- Firms need to be able to show who was responsible for any areas of the business, at any point in time, through a Responsibilities Map. The Responsibilities Map should be auditable, comprehensive, and up to date.

Breach reporting

- Any breach of the Conduct Rules by senior managers under the SMR will need to be reported within seven days of a firm encountering the actual or suspected breach. All other actual or suspected breaches by staff who are subject to the Conduct Rules will need to be reported on an aggregate annual basis.

The role of non-executive directors

- Only certain non-executive directors will be affected by the Senior Managers Regime (SMR). Any regulatory related challenges brought to the executive by non-executive directors will need to be evidenced clearly.

Authorising Firms

Permissions

- Smaller Firms must apply to the FCA for permission to carry out any regulated activities.
- Larger firms apply to the PRA
- Authorisation is not necessary if the firm is exempt.

Exempt Persons

- Appointed Representatives (ARs) are exempt so long as the provider firm, known as the principle, takes full responsibility for the representative
- AR's can be introducers or able to give advice.
- Certain institutions such as local government and central banks – Bank of England and the European Central Bank.
- Exempt professional firms
    - Members of professions such as lawyers and accountants.
    - They have to obtain permission from the FCA to carry out any regulated activities if the business is mainstream.
    - They are exempt if the business is non-mainstream.
    - These firms are known as designated professional bodies.

Responsibilities of Regulated Firms

- Authorised firms are responsible for the conduct of their employees, agents and ARs.
- Firms must have systems in place:
  - Senior Management Systems and Controls
  - Proper internal procedures are drawn up to protect firms.
  - Policies drawn up to describe how risks are controlled.
  - Audit systems and records in place.
  - Whistle Blowing - firms must make it easy for staff to blow the whistle on any suspicious activities.
  - Compliance Officers
    - Firms must appoint someone to this role and are a controlled function.
    - Their responsibilities are:
      - To maintain a compliance manual.
      - Keeping records on financial promotions and complaints.
      - Deal with the FCA.
      - Be responsible for the T&C Scheme and selling practices of the firm.

"THE BOSS TURNED DOWN MY OFFER TO COORDINATE THE OFFICE AGAIN."

Adviser Status

Independent advice

- An Independent Financial Adviser (IFA) represents the client.
- Advice is "unrestricted and unbiased"
- The IFA's firm or network is responsible for their actions.
- Many operate a "panel" of carefully chosen providers
- IFAs operate on a fee basis since 2012

Restricted advice

- Acts on behalf of the provider and can only advise on one or a selection of provider's own products.
- The firm is responsible for all actions of the adviser

Retail Distribution Review

Clarity of Service

- With effect from 2013
- Firms act in the best interests of their customers distinguishing between selling and advising.
- Advice provided by Independent Financial Advisers
- Advisers must choose between giving:
  - Independent advice
  - Restricted advice – ranges from single tie to multi-tie

Remuneration

- Charges for advice are set with no provider involvement
- The charging policy and "tariff" set and supplied to customers before any meeting
- No variations dependent on provider although it may be appropriate for some product types

Professional Standards

- Minimum level of qualification raised to QCA Level 4
- Accredited bodies created to monitor and CPD activities enhanced

Supervising Firms

Judgement Based Supervision

- The previous regulator, the FSA used the principle of "risk based" supervision, spending their time and resources on firms who portrayed the highest risk.

- The new FCA wish to be able to act quicker and uses judgement based supervision.

- The FCA will work closely with senior members of management teams, get to grips with strategy and direction and will make a judgement early on as to whether the consumer is going to be adversely affected.

- It categorises firms:
    - C1 – large banks and insurance groups
    - C2 – firms with substantial retail customers
    - C3 – firms with a large client base
    - C4 – smaller firms, most brokers and intermediaries.

- Supervision, time and effort, is based on their category – C1 firms getting closer supervision than C4.

- It uses three pillars:
    - Preventative work with firms
    - Event driven work
    - Issue and products

Compliance Monitoring

- The FCA receives a constant flow of information from firms such as auditor statements, business volumes, sources of business, complaints statistics.
- They will then react to these metrics.
- The FCA is also proactive and has a programme of visits and contact via its enforcement officers.
- These visits look at business operations, personal matters and customer matters.
- Mystery shopping activities are also conducted.

Financial Strength

- Measuring the strength of life offices and firms is vital to the FCA.
- Banks and building Societies show their strength via the returns they offer
- Life offices have free asset ratio which is the surplus assets held over the value of its liabilities.
- IFAs will look closely at this figure before recommending an office to clients.
- Ratings, such as Fitch and Standard and Poors, are also used to assess strength of offices and firms.

The Regulation of Financial Services

FCA's Enforcement Powers

- The FCA has powers to investigate any firm with no barriers, known as enforcement.
- It can then impose disciplinary action, in order of severity:
    - Restrict their product selling, a variation of their permissions
    - Stop them trading altogether.
    - Injunction i.e. freezes assets.
    - Restitution i.e. pass on profit to the FCA if this was gained via a contravention of a regulation
    - Redress - order the firm to compensate customers e.g. endowment mis-selling.
    - Discipline them i.e. publicise their wrong doing or fine them.

Mortgage Market Review

- The first major change in the mortgage since 2005 brought upon by the Credit Crunch and the main blame being laid against irresponsible lending.

- The main points are:

    - Income will have to be verified in every mortgage application – bringing an end to both self-certification and to fast-track mortgage products.

    - The rules for determining disposable income, to support affordability, are less prescriptive than originally proposed, but guidance on what lenders should consider is provided.

    - Lenders will have to decide on the "stress test" they wish to apply, to check that mortgage applicants will be able to afford the payments should interest rates rise.

    - Interest only mortgages will still be permitted, but lenders will have to satisfy themselves that the borrower has a credible strategy to repay the capital at the end of the term.

    - The vast majority of sales will have to be carried out on an advised basis – all sales where there is human interaction, face to face, phone or e mail, will have to be advised.

    - Mortgage Professionals and certified High Net Worth individuals will be able to proceed on an execution only basis.

    - Certain mortgage applicants who pose a higher risk to themselves, such as those consolidating debts, will have to get explicit advice.

    - And there will be special transitional rules for borrowers caught by changes in rules – the so called "mortgage prisoners" – and both their existing lender or a new lender can apply transitional rules to ensure they're not disadvantaged if they wish to move home or re-mortgage.

6 FCA Rules for Firms

Financial Promotions

- The rules regarding prospecting are entitled "Financial Promotions". They draw a distinction between "written" and "non-written".

- Non-Written financial promotions are a personal visit, telephone conversation, or other dialogue. Also known as real time.

- Written financial promotions are those made by email, letter, appearing in newspapers, on TV or website. Also known as non-real time.

- Unsolicited real time, known as cold calling, mustn't be conducted unless the customer has a relationship with the firm or the promotion is a low risk product. The call must be made at an appropriate time of the day i.e. 9am to 9pm Monday to Saturday.

Advertising

- Advertising rules cover publications, circulars, catalogues, posters, radio, television, as well as business cards and letterheads.
- Contents of all adverts must be approved by an authorised person.
  - A specific individual must be nominated to assume responsibility for checking adverts.
- All advertisements must:
  - Be clear and fair in what is stated and what is implied;
  - Have regard to the likely sophistication of the reader;
  - Observe the rules of the Advertising Standards Authority;
  - Clearly state the tax implications;
  - Show the name of the regulatory body (and for tied agents the name of the company to whom tied).
- If past performance is quoted, adverts must:
  - Quote the source of the figures;
  - State that past performance is not necessarily a guide to the future, and that the value can go down as well as up;
  - At least 5 years of figures to be used.
- Business cards must show:
  - Adviser's name and company represented;
  - Business address and telephone number;
  - The regulatory body through which he/she is authorised.
- All business documents and letterheads must show clearly which regulatory body has authorised the firm.

Reporting and Record Keeping

Record keeping

- All records of pension transfers, pension opt outs and FSAVCs to be kept indefinitely
- All records for:
  - Life and pension contracts – 5 years
  - MiFID – 5 years
  - All other contracts – 3 years
  - Training and Competence Records – 3 years after they have left the firm
- Advertising records to be kept:
  - Pensions transfers, pension opt outs and FSAVCs – Indefinitely
  - Life and pensions – 6 years
  - MiFID – 5 years
  - All other – 3 years

Reporting Rules

- Electronic reporting via GABRIEL
- Regular returns required by FCA

Training and Competence

The firm's commitment

- The firm's commitment to training and competence should be that employees:
    - Are competent;
    - Remain competent;
    - Are appropriately supervised;
    - Have competence reviewed regularly;
    - Have level of competence appropriate to the business.

Recruitment

- In recruitment for specified roles involving private customers, including giving investment advice, the firm must:
    - Take account of an individual's knowledge and skill for the role;
    - Find out about the individual's previous relevant activities and training;

Training

- For advisers and other employees involved with private customers, the firm must determine training needs and organise appropriate timely training.

Attaining competence

- Employees must pass appropriate examinations before being assessed as competent. Otherwise, the employee may only engage in the relevant activity under appropriate supervision.

- Employees permitted to work with private customers under supervision must first have passed the relevant regulatory module of an appropriate examination. On-the-job training is not sufficient.

- The time which may be spent under supervision before taking approved exams is 30 months.

- For certain specialist advice, such as advice on pension transfers, these are specific exam requirements before the employee can engage in the activity.

Maintaining competence

- Firms must ensure that employees maintain competence in their activities, for example through Continuing Professional Development (CPD).

- Now prescribed at a minimum of 35 hours in each 12 month period, 21 of which must be structured.

Supervision

- Employees who are not yet assessed as competent in an activity need to be appropriately supervised.

- Supervisors of those giving advice on packaged products must have passed an appropriate examination and must have the technical knowledge and assessment and coaching skills to act as a supervisor.

Record keeping

- Appropriate records must be retained for at least three years after the employee leaves the firm although, for pension transfer specialists, records must be retained indefinitely.

Appropriate examinations

- The new regulatory regime covers a wide range of activities within the financial sector previously covered by different regulators, and lists of appropriate examinations, apply.

- 'Back office' employees overseeing administrative functions such as dealing with client money or taking private customers through decision trees must pass examinations within 30 months.

"HAVE YOU HAD ANY LEADERSHIP EXPERIENCE OTHER THAN HAVING A DOG?"

7 FCA Conduct of Business Rules

Types of Client

Know Your Client

- The rules require that all advisers must get to "know their client".
- The majority of companies use a factfind to demonstrate this. Factfinds vary from firm to firm and as a guidance, the FCA distinguish types of customer.

Retail Client

- Most clients.
- The man on the street who requires most protection.

Professional Client

- This category provides some level of investor protection where the firm feels it is better protected by giving more advice.
- People expected to have a level of understanding.

Eligible Counterparty

- Institutions, banks, investment firms and governments.
- Usually goes with execution-only transactions.

Status Disclosure with clients

- All advisers must have a written agreement with every client, setting out their business relationship.

Client Agreement

- Required when a firm provides high risk investment business such as discretionary fund management
- Not required with packaged investments and low ticket items
- This must cover:
    - Contact details and how the firm will maintain contact
    - The full name of the adviser's regulator.
    - Details of the investment services offered, in particular whether they handle client money.
    - The status of the adviser – independent of restricted – if restricted, the nature of the restriction
    - How the adviser is remunerated.
    - Withdrawal rights.
    - Complaints processes.

Discretionary management agreement

- Some clients wish to give their advisers even more discretion to invest on their behalf. In that case, the agreement must set out, in addition to the above, the limitations of discretion within which the adviser/manager must operate.

FCA Conduct of Business Rules

Services and Costs Disclosure Document (SCDD)

- This document set out the key facts about the firm and its services in a standard format.
- Includes
    - The types of products offered;
    - Whether the products are sourced from the whole market;
    - Whether advice and recommendation is provided;
    - Whether payment is required for the service;
    - Details of ownership and regulation;
    - How to complain to the company, and if not satisfied, to the Financial Ombudsman Service;
    - How to obtain compensation from the Financial Services Compensation Scheme.

Client Money

Client Assets

- Rules to safeguard client assets from being mixed with firm's assets.

- Designed to prevent these being included in firm's assets for example, in event of insolvency.

Client Money Rules

- Apply to firms who receive or hold client's money.

- They don't apply to banks, Building Societies or life offices.

- A firm must hold their client's money separately in a client bank account in the name of the client.

- Interest belongs to the client.

- Most IFAs receive cheques payable to the life office so don't fall under these rules.

FCA Conduct of Business Rules

Suitability Requirements

- You cannot give advice on any regulated product until you have fully ascertained the client's personal and financial circumstances.
- Factfinds are the answer and these were covered in detail in the previous section.
- Risk is a major factor and clients must be made aware of any risks the product may have.
- Factfinds must be kept for:
  - Indefinitely if pension transfer or FSAVC business was transacted.
  - 5 years for life and pension business.
  - 3 years for other products.

"I'M AFRAID WE'VE HAD AN ERROR CREEP INTO LAST WEEKS' CLASS ON 'HOW TO GET YOUR FOOT IN THE DOOR'."

Suitable Recommendation

- Recommendations must be purely in the client's best interests, and must not be influenced by the adviser's interests - such as the amount of commission.
- It must be based on a thorough understanding of the client's needs and objectives, through a factfind.
- If client declines to supply relevant information, note this down and take particular care in recommendations.
- Advisers must take all reasonable steps to ensure the client understands the risks of the advice and must obtain the client's risk profile.

Suitability Reports

- A suitability report is required following a personal recommendation to a retain customer on:
  - A life policy.
  - A pension plan.
  - Pensions transfers and opt outs.
  - Unit trusts, OEICs, Investment Trusts.
- Not required for mortgage advice
- The suitability letter explains why the firm has concluded that the transaction is suitable, given the customer's circumstances.

FCA Conduct of Business Rules

Executions

Best Execution

- Ensuring that a transaction for a client is done on the best terms available at the time for transactions of that nature and size.
- Applies particularly to buying and selling of stocks and shares.
- Does not apply to life assurance and pensions, or to unit trusts.

Execution only

- An "execution only" transaction occurs when a client instructs the adviser to carry out a specific investment deal on his behalf without requiring or receiving any advice of any kind.
- The client therefore acts entirely on his own responsibility. The adviser's usual duty of care does not apply.
- The adviser must obtain the client's signed confirmation that a transaction is execution only.

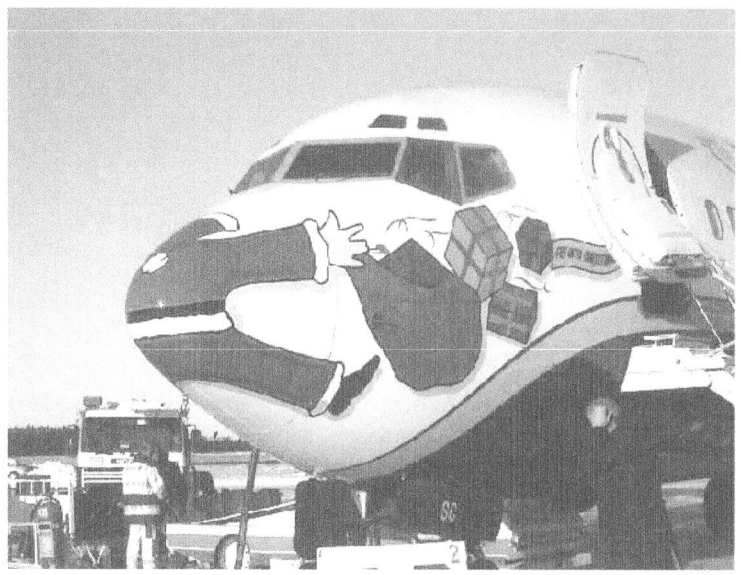

Cancellation

- Known as the "cooling off" notice.
- The post-sale notice is accompanied by a slip or form, or electronic equivalent, enabling the customer to exercise the right to cancel.
- The cooling off period is normally 14 days from the receipt by the client of a "cancellation notice" issued by the product provider direct to the client. Products which have a 14 day cooling off period are:
  - Cash ISAs
  - Unit Trusts/OEICs
  - CTFs
  - ISAs
  - EISs
  - Designated investments
- Products with a 30 day cooling off period are:
  - Life polices
  - Personal Pensions
  - Stakeholder Pensions
  - Pension transfers
- The client can withdraw from the contract at any time during this period without any commitment or loss.
- The only exception is when a client has invested in a unit linked investment product where the value of units has fallen during the cancellation period.
- This "fall" will be reflected in the cancellation value.

Product Disclosure

Key Features Document

- Product providers must produce a key features document for each of its packaged products.
- Hard copy or electronic.
- Given before the application is completed
- Contents of document:
  - Nature of investment
  - Risk of the product
  - Cancellation rights
  - Complaints procedure
  - Product details – sums, premiums
  - Surrender implications

Projection Rules

- When a projection is produced, the rules must be followed.
- Based on reasonable assumptions

With Profits

- Life offices must have a Principles and Practices of Financial Management document which sets out how they manage the with profit fund.
- Must be sent to policy holders annually

CeMAP 1 Revision Guide

Stakeholder Products

- The Government has striven to make financial products easy to understand and good value.
- The suite of Stakeholder style products are:
    - Cash deposit like an ISA;
    - A collective investment like an OEIC;
    - An "smoothed" investment similar to a With Profits scheme;
    - The Stakeholder Pension;
    - The Child Trust Fund and Junior ISA;
- Many of the Conduct of Business Rules are greatly simplified for Stakeholder products. This is known as Basic Advice.

"WE'RE LIVING IN A WORLD OF LOWERED EXPECTATIONS."

Types of Advice

Basic advice

- Basic advice is a limited form of advice focussing on one or more needs.
- Doesn't involve in depth factfinding.
- Firm must provide a "basic advice initial disclosure document"
- The sales process must use only Stakeholder products with pre-scripted questions.
- The client must understand the nature of the product and records kept for 5 years
- Although many sales processes are automated, there needs to be a competent adviser on hand to answer questions.

Generic advice

- Covers advice on general matters without the characteristics of basic advice

Focussed advice

- At request of customer, focusses on specific need area

Simplified advice

- Limited to one or two areas of need with a specific factfind.

Regulation of Mortgage Advice

How are mortgages regulated

- Mortgages became regulated from October 2004.
- Covers loans taken by individuals with first charges taken.
- The property must be in the UK and be at least 40% lived in by the borrower or family.
- Rules cover most aspects – lending, administration, and advice.
- All lenders and intermediaries need authorisation.
- Mortgage sales must occur on an advice basis or an information only basis with no advice.
- Advice requirements ensure that:
  - The customer can afford the loan, now and in the future;
  - That a mortgage is indeed suitable;
  - The most suitable type of mortgage and mortgage product is selected;
  - The most suitable lender is chosen.

Buy to Let Mortgages

- Previously Buy to Let mortgages were not regulated by the FCA since they fall outside of the 40% rule and are generally not lived in by family members.

- This has now changed with the FCA preferring to distinguish between:
    - Buy to Let mortgages arranged by a business and
    - Buy to Let mortgage arranged by an individual or consumer

- They're regulating the one arranged by a consumer but not the one organised by a business. The vast majority of professional landlords who use Buy to Let mortgages to build up their property portfolios, do so via a company of some sort to minimise taxation.

- The FCA recognises that some people inherit a buy to let mortgage with a let to buy, where their existing home is rented out on a temporary basis whilst they live elsewhere. These people need protection and the mortgage needs to be regulated. Providers of these will have to adhere to the MCOBs from now on.

Second Charge Lending

- In a similar manner to Buy to Lets, 2nd Charge Lending is now under the guidance of the FCA and providers must adhere to the MCOBs.

- And rightly so. They are dealing with consumers, often arranging large sums on the security of residential homes. They offer slightly easier lending terms with the ubiquitous higher interest rates.

- So rather than be regulated by the new CONC, which provide the rules for firms involved in the consumer credit market, providers are pretty much on par with first charge mortgage lenders.

Disclosure

- Initial disclosure document.
    - Given out on the first client meeting and outlines the services offered.
    - No longer a requirement to issue a written IDD for non-distance mortgage contracts such as face to face sales, you have to give the "key messages" verbally and document on the file that disclosure has been given.
- Key Facts Illustration.
    - Given before the application form completed.
    - Similar to the KFD in that product details are easily compared. Like for like.
    - Given for further advance lending and transfer of equity (removing or adding another person to the mortgage).
- Offer document.
    - Produced by the lender.
    - Up to date KFI issued as well.
- Lifetime mortgages (home income plans) require additional documentation to safeguard the customer.

Unfair practices

- Mortgage cold call selling will not be allowed.
- Excessive fees will not be permitted.
- Key Facts Illustrations must illustrate fees.
- All mortgage arrangement fees must be included in APR.

Training & Competence

- Advisers must adhere to the normal T&C requirements unless already competent.
- Additional training required for lifetime mortgages.

Complaints and Compensation

- Lenders and intermediaries fall under Financial Ombudsman Service and Compensation Scheme.

FCA Conduct of Business Rules

MCOB Summary

MCOB 1	Application and Purpose	• Helps firms understand which parts of the MCOB rules apply to them provides guidance on the application of other parts of the FCA Handbook
MCOB 2	Conduct of Business Standards: General	• General requirements that apply throughout the mortgage sourcebook • Communications must be clear fair and not misleading • Rules on inducements
MCOB 3	Financial Promotions	• Content requirements for qualifying credit promotions • Rules banning unsolicited real-time promotions (cold calling)
MCOB 4	Advising and Selling Standards	• The initial disclosure document • Independence • Suitability of advice • Non-advised sales
MCOB 5	Pre-application disclosure	• Timing and content of the key facts illustration (KFI)
MCOB 6	Disclosure at offer stage	• Content of the offer document
MCOB 7	Disclosure at Start of Contract and After Sale	• Start of contract information requirements • Annual statements • Information requirements for post-sale contract variations (such as further advances)
MCOB 8	Equity Release: Advising and Selling Standards	• A tailored regime for advising and selling lifetime mortgages
MCOB 9	Equity Release: Product Disclosure	• Tailored product disclosure requirements for lifetime mortgages
MCOB 10	Annual Percentage Rate	• How to calculate the APR
MCOB 11	Responsible Lending	• Requirement for lenders to check the consumer's ability to repay
MCOB 12	Charges	• Charges in key areas (for example, arrears and early repayment charges) must be reasonable, based on the cost to the lender • Charges must not be excessive
MCOB 13	Arrears and Repossessions	• Information requirements for fair treatment of borrowers in arrears and facing repossession

CeMAP 1 Revision Guide

ICOBS

FSA factsheet for

Insurance brokers

ICOBS at a glance – highlights of the new rules

Rules (R) and guidance (G) – applies to all firms, all products, and both consumers and commercial customers unless otherwise stated.

Other rules apply to protection products in addition to or instead of these rules – see overleaf.

Status disclosure	(R) An insurance intermediary must at least provide the customer with specified details about itself and its complaints procedure (IMD information). This can be given in a durable medium or, in certain circumstances orally, or limited information can be given according to the DMD telephone sale rules. If the information is provided orally, written information must be provided immediately after the conclusion of the contract. An IDD may be used to satisfy status disclosure if it is used in accordance with its notes and provided to the customer at the correct time. (R) Insurers and intermediaries must disclose fees.
Suitability	(R) Based on Principle 9 - A firm must take reasonable care to ensure the suitability of its advice for any customer who is entitled to rely on its judgement.
Eligibility & disclosure of material facts	(G) A firm should take reasonable steps to ensure a customer only buys a policy under which he is eligible to claim benefits. A firm should tell the customer, if it finds out at any time while arranging a policy, that parts of the cover do not apply. (G) Guidance is set out outlining ways a firm can ensure a customer knows what he should disclose as regards material facts.
Product disclosure	(R) A firm must take reasonable steps to ensure a customer is given appropriate information about a policy in good time and in a comprehensible form so that the customer can make an informed decision about the arrangements proposed. (G) The information required will vary and, for example, depend on: • the knowledge, experience and ability of a typical customer; • the policy terms, including main benefits, exclusions and limitations, conditions and duration; • the policy's overall complexity; • whether the policy is bought in connection with other goods and services; • distance communications information requirements; and • whether the same information has been provided to the customer previously and, if so, when. (G) A policy summary is optional.
Price disclosure	(G) The high level product disclosure rule also applies to disclosing the price of the policy. (R) Separate price disclosure of the premium and whether buying the policy is compulsory is required for all secondary sales.
Cancellation	(R) Consumers have a right, with some exceptions, to cancel a general insurance policy within 14 days (for PPI – see overleaf) for any reason and without penalty. However, the firm can retain an amount for the service already provided in accordance with the contract.
Claims handling	(R) Insurers must: • handle claims promptly and fairly; • provide reasonable guidance to help policyholders make a claim; • not unreasonably reject a claim; and • settle claims promptly once settlement terms are agreed. (R) Insurers should not reject a claim by a consumer if the claim is due to: • non-disclosure of a fact material to the risk which the policyholder could not reasonably have been expected to have disclosed; • non-negligent misrepresentation of a fact material to the risk; or • a breach of a warranty or condition unrelated to the claim.

ICOBS at a glance – highlights of the new rules

FCA Conduct of Business Rules

FSA factsheet for Insurance brokers

ICOBS at a glance – highlights (continued)

Requirements for protection products - pure protection contracts and payment protection policies (PPI) – or, where indicated, solely for PPI.

These apply in addition to or instead of the requirements overleaf.

Status disclosure	(R) All firms - in a non-advised sale, a firm must take steps to ensure the customer understands that he is responsible for deciding if a policy meets his demands and needs. If a firm provides information orally on a main characteristic of a policy, it must take reasonable steps to explain the customer's responsibility orally.
	(R) Insurers - must disclose at least the name of the regulator, whose policies they offer, and whether they are providing a personal recommendation or information.
	(R) Intermediaries – same as overleaf
	(R) All firms - if part of the status information is delivered orally, all elements must be delivered orally.
Suitability	(G) In an advised sale, a firm should obtain relevant information to determine demands and needs and take into account existing cover, the level of cover provided by the policy, cost, relevant exclusions and conditions. It should tell the customer of any demands and needs not met. In a non-advised sale the firm would also need to give a customer a record of all his demands and needs that have been discussed and provide a key features document.
Eligibility & disclosure of material facts	(R) A firm arranging a PPI policy must take reasonable steps to ensure a customer only buys a policy under which he is eligible to claim benefits. The firm must tell the customer, if it finds out when arranging the policy, that parts of the cover do not apply.
Product disclosure	(R) If a firm provides any information orally to a customer on a main characteristic of a policy, it must do so for all of the policy's main characteristics.
	(R) A firm must take reasonable steps to ensure the information provided orally is sufficient to enable the customer to take an informed decision without overloading the customer or obscuring other parts of the information.
	(R) A policy summary is required in good time before the conclusion of the contract.
	(R) A firm must draw a consumer's attention to reading PPI documentation before the end of the cancellation period to check it is suitable. This information must be given orally if a firm provides information orally on a main characteristic of the policy.
Price disclosure	(R) A firm must provide price information in a way calculated to enable the customer to relate it to a regular budget.
	(G) Price information is considered a main characteristic of the policy, so must be provided orally if another main characteristic is disclosed orally.
	(R) Premiums paid using a non-revolving credit agreement, e.g. single premium PPI, must be disclosed in a way calculated to enable the customer to understand the total cost of the policy and the additional repayments that relate to the purchase of the policy.
	(G) Price information for policies sold with revolving credit should enable a typical customer to understand the typical cumulative cost of the policy.
Cancellation	(R) Consumers have a right to cancel pure protection contracts and all PPI contracts (not just those with a life insurance element) within 30 days for any reason and without penalty. They can obtain a full refund of premium for pure protection contracts. They can obtain a full refund for PPI contracts unless a claim has been made within the cancellation period and settlement terms are subsequently agreed.
Claims handling	No additional requirements.

Note: This is a summary of the main requirements within ICOBS but it does not include the totality of the requirements for all firms. Firms must refer to the FSA Handbook to ensure that they are aware of and in compliance with all the rules applicable to them. There are variations to the requirements and timing of information for sales by telephone and internet. In addition, different provisions may apply depending on the type of customer with whom a firm is dealing.

ICOBS at a glance – highlights of the new rules

8 Consumer Credit Regulation

FCA Regulation of Consumer Credit

- Replaced the OFT – Office of Fair Training – and has wider enforcement powers.
- FCA authorises:
  - Consumer credit lending
  - Credit broking
  - Debt counselling and collection
  - Credit information services
  - Credit reference agencies
- FCA now enforces Consumer Credit Acts
  - FCA Conduct rules apply
  - Treating customers fairly applies
  - Authorisation process adapting
  - Approved person regime applies
  - Full investigation, enforcement and redress

Consumer Credit Sourcebook CONC

CONC 1	Application and purpose and guidance on financial difficulties
CONC 2	Conduct of business standards: general
CONC 3	Financial promotions and communications with customers
CONC 4	Pre-contractual requirements
CONC 5	Responsible lending
CONC 5A	Cost cap for high-cost short-term credit
CONC 6	Post contractual requirements
CONC 7	Arrears, default and recovery (including repossessions)
CONC 8	Debt advice
CONC 9	Credit reference agencies
CONC 10	Prudential rules for debt management firms
CONC 11	Cancellation
CONC 12	Requirements for firms with interim permission for credit-related regulated activities
CONC 13	Guidance on the duty to give information under sections 77, 78 and 79 of the Consumer Credit Act 1974
CONC 14	Requirement in relation to agents
CONC 15	Second charge lending

Consumer Credit Acts

Consumer Credit Act 1974

- This Act regulated loan agreements, quotations and advertisements, and other activities of lenders and credit reference agencies.

- It applies to "Consumer Credit Agreements" which are basically loans and other forms of credit with no upper limit.

- Suppliers of credit as defined in the act must be licensed by the Office of Fair Trading.

- Typical Annual Percentage Rate (APR) must be shown. APRs include the interest charge plus all the compulsory charges to give a balanced view of the total charge.

- Clients must be made aware of :
  - The nature of the contract;
  - Their rights and obligations.

- Clients must receive a copy of a loan agreement for their own records.

- Loan agreements must contain cooling off provisions unless they are signed on the lenders premises.

- Credit reference agencies must disclose information held, and must correct it if inaccurate.

Consumer Credit Act 2006

- Financial Ombudsman Service incorporates all consumer credit disputes.

- Borrowers can now challenge credit agreements in Court.

- No upper limit for the size of the loan – used to be £25,000.

- Lenders to provide more information throughout the term of the loan.

Consumer Credit (Advertisement) Regulations 2004

- Make things fairer for consumers and encourages a more competitive market.
- Looks at:
  - Advertisements for credit;
  - Simpler agreements for customers to sign;
  - More disclosure;
  - Fairer early redemption charges.

The EU Consumer Credit Directive

- The Directive has been implemented in the UK under the Consumer Credit Regulations 2010. These provide:
- Changes on the right to withdraw and providing adequate explanations. A 14 day withdrawal is allowed.
- New assumptions for calculating APR.
- Provides new and clearer information to be given to consumers prior to entering an agreement
- New requirements of information to be included in an agreement
- Sets out advertising requirements particularly how the APR is quoted

Consumer Rights Legislation

The Consumer Rights Act 2015

- Supersedes previous legislation.
- Gives enhanced rights to consumers with faulty goods and services.
- Act covers:
  - What to do when goods are faulty
  - How services should be fit for purpose
  - Faulty provision of goods and services
  - Unfair terms in contracts
  - How organisations can respond to breaches of law
- The act aims to reduce time involved in dealing with consumer disputes
- Third party arbitrator can be asked to make decision about disputes, in a similar manner to FOS.

Unfair Contract Terms

- Previous legislation has been revoked by Consumer Rights Act 2015
- The following provisions are included in all such contracts:
  - The service will be performed with reasonable care;
  - The work will be done within a reasonable time;
  - A reasonable charge will be made.
- Affects contracts between suppliers and the consumer where the contract used is a standard one and not tailored.
- For example a new home builder using their standard contract for sale but not an individual selling their own home where a tailored contract would be used.
  - The regulations covers fairness, usage of plain language and good faith.

Advertising Codes and Guidelines

- The Advertising Code
  - This Code is prepared by representatives of the various associations of advertisers, agencies and media owners.
  - All advertisements should be legal, decent, honest and truthful.
  - All advertisements should be prepared with a sense of responsibility to the consumer and to society.
- Advertising Standards Authority
  - The ASA is financed by a surcharge on display advertising and monitors compliance with the British Code of Advertising Practice and the Code of Sales Promotion Practice.
  - Advertising must be legal, decent, honest and truthful.
  - The ASA receives complaints and ensures that offensive, misleading or dishonest advertisements are withdrawn.

Competition and Markets Authority

- Independent body ensuring healthy competition in the UK.

- They are responsible for:
    - investigating mergers which could restrict competition
    - conducting market studies and investigations in markets where there may be competition and consumer problems
    - investigating where there may be breaches of UK or EU prohibitions against anti-competitive agreements and abuses of dominant positions
    - bringing criminal proceedings against individuals who commit the cartel offence
    - enforcing consumer protection legislation to tackle practices and market conditions that make it difficult for consumers to exercise choice
    - co-operating with sector regulators and encouraging them to use their competition powers
    - considering regulatory references and appeals

STAFF NOTICE

Due to escalating costs, increased competition and a keen desire to stay in Business it is necessary to change our terms of employment. It will now be necessary to do something called work in between the coffee breaks, lunch breaks, tea breaks, smoking breaks, toilet breaks etc. It is the management intention to call this

THE WORK BREAK

9 Complaints and Disputes

- The rules require firms to deal properly and promptly with consumer complaints.
- The key requirements for firms' complaint handling procedures are that firms must:
  - Have appropriate and effective internal complaints handling procedures;
  - Make consumers aware of those procedures;
  - Ensure the complainant is kept informed thereafter of the progress of the measures being taken for the complaint's resolution
  - Aim to resolve complaints within 8 weeks;
  - Notify complainants of their right to go to the Financial Ombudsman Service if they are not satisfied;
  - Report information about their complaints handling to the FCA on a regular six-monthly basis;
  - Maintain records for at least 3 years. MiFID and UCITs – 5 years.

"CERTAINLY THAT'S OUR WARRANTY, BUT NOTHING WENT WRONG WHILE WE HAD IT SIR..."

The Financial Ombudsman Service

- The concept of an ombudsman, as a person (or more often these days an organisation) providing an independent facility for the resolution of complaints and disputes relating to public bodies and commercial organisations, has been with us for many years.

- It has 3 divisions.
    - Banking and loan division.
    - Insurance Division.
    - Investment Division.

- The Pensions Ombudsman is a separate concern.
    - Deals with complaints about the running of pension schemes.
    - Complaints surrounding advice from an adviser will go to the Financial Services Ombudsman.

Ombudsman's Rules

- It is compulsory for all authorised firms to be members of the FOS.

- Access to the FOS is open to all private individuals and to small businesses (i.e. those with an annual turnover of less than 2 million Euros).

- The Ombudsman can make awards of up to £150,000. The aim of the awards is to put customers back in the position they would have been in if things had not gone wrong.

- Individuals must first complain to the firm itself. Only when a firm's own internal complaints procedure has been exhausted without the customer obtaining satisfaction can the FOS be approached.

- Complaints must be made to the FOS within 6 months of the customer receiving a letter from the firm setting out its final decision on the complaint. This is sometimes known as a "deadlock" letter.

- The Ombudsman's initial approach will often be to attempt mediation between customer and firm by suggesting a way of resolution. Only if the parties do not agree on this will a formal investigation be commenced.

- Decisions and awards by the Ombudsman are binding on member firms, but not on customers, who are always free to go to court instead.

Financial Services Compensation Scheme

- The scheme is made up of a number of sub-schemes relating to different default situations, as follows:

Insolvency

- Loss due to insolvency of a firm carrying out investment business – 100% of the first £50,000
- This also includes mortgage claims

Insurance Company default

- Default of an insurance company: compensation of 90% of the value of the policy.
- Compulsory insurance ensures 100% of the value of the policy i.e. motor third party insurance.

Loss of deposits

- Loss of deposited funds due to the default of a bank or building society – 100 per cent of the first £85,000 of each depositor's claim.
- £75,000 from January 1, 2016, part of a recalibration of the threshold following falls in the euro against the pound.
- Up to £1 million for temporary high balances such as proceeds from a house sale or divorce settlement.

Mortgage Firms

- Claims against mortgage firms for inappropriate advice – 100% of up to £50,000; where the firm is unable to pay claims against it.

Investment company is in default

A CHELTENHAM investment company has been declared in default by the Financial Services Compensation Scheme.

Customers of Regal Elite Services, which traded as the Pensions and Investment Centre in Berkeley Mews, could now be entitled to up to £48,000 in compensation.

The firm operated between March 1993 and October 2000 and was formerly known as Regal & Universal Investments (UK) Limited.

The FSCS has declared the firm in default because it can't pay existing claims.

One outstanding claim against the firm is estimated at more than £14,000.

Esther Norris, communications officer for the FSCS, urged people to find out if they could get compensation.

She said: "The firm operated for some time so many people could be suffering unnecessarily. We're asking them to claim what they're entitled to."

People who believe they may have a claim should contact the Scheme on 020 7892 7300.

■ Have you had problems with Regal Elite Services? Please call the Echo newsdesk on 01242 271820.

10 Money Laundering

Introduction

- Massively high profile issue.
- Financial crime includes money laundering, insider trading, funding of terrorism.
- Financial Action Task Force – international body with 36 member countries.
- National Crime Agency is the UK intelligence agency that looks after money laundering in the UK.

Proceeds of Crime Act 2002

- Now deals with all sorts of crime.
- Consolidates all previous legislation.

Terrorism Act 2000

- Act criminalises the holding of terrorists property. Includes terrorist's money, assets, and proceeds of terrorism.

European Directives

- 3rd Money Laundering Directive aims to define money laundering.
  - Converting property into laundered cash
  - Concealing true origins of cash.
  - Acquiring property from financial crime.
  - Participating with money launderers.
- Property is pretty much everything that you can see and can't physically touch such as title deeds.
- Criminal property is defined and property knowingly derived from criminal activities.

Rules for Authorised Firms

- Establish procedures to deal with money laundering.

- Appoint a Money Laundering Reporting Officer, a controlled function who must produce a minimum of a monthly report of all suspicions reported and liaise with the National Crime Agency.

- Train staff.
    - Aware of procedures.
    - Recognise money laundering.
    - Knows the Money Laundering Reporting Officer.
    - Personal consequences if they don't adhere to the rules.

- Obtain Identification from customers.

- Include passport, driving license, utility bill.

- Customers without ID can be excluded from the product purely because they don't have necessary ID.

- Report suspicious activity. Failure to disclose this is a criminal activity.

- Not to alert suspicious customers or "tip" them off.

- Continually strengthen procedures.

Offences

- Concealing criminal property.
- Arranging i.e. getting involved in the laundering process.
- Acquiring or using criminal property.
- Severe penalties under Money Laundering Regulations 2003.
  - Unlimited fines.
  - Up to 14 years in prison.

Record Keeping

- ID evidence kept for 5 years following the end of the customer relationship.
- Any supporting evidence to be kept for 5 years.

11 Data Protection

Data Protection Act 1998

- This Act deals with the control, handling and use of information about individuals held on computer, paper-based and other manually held information.

- All businesses holding information about individuals on computer must register.

- It introduces the concept of "sensitive data" (about race, sexual behaviour or physical or mental health) and requires explicit consent to be given for the use of such data.

"...PSST, HEY BUDDY! USED MAILING LISTS?"

Data Protection

8 Principles

1. Data held must be used in a lawful manner, and not used in any manner other than that for which it is kept.

2. It may not be held for longer than necessary to complete the purpose for which it was originally obtained.

3. It must be adequate and relevant for that purpose, but not excessive.

4. It must be kept accurate and up-to-date. If incorrect it must be corrected when the inaccuracy is pointed out.

5. It may not be disclosed to anyone not connected with its purpose.

6. It must be kept securely, and not be accessible by unauthorised persons.

7. An individual must be given access to data about himself at a cost of £10 which mustn't take longer than 40 days.

8. Data cannot be transferred out of the EU, unless the country to which it is sent has adequate data protection legislation.

Enforcement

- Information Commissioners oversee act.
- They can serve enforcement on firms if they infringe the act.

CeMAP 1 Revision Guide

EU Data Protection Directive

EU DATA PROTECTION DIRECTIVE

How Prepared Are You?

Data Protection is already a priority for businesses, but the revision to the EU Data Protection Regulation coming into effect in 2015 is set to raise the stakes even higher ...

THREE IMPORTANT THINGS YOU NEED TO KNOW ABOUT THE IMPENDING LEGISLATION

1. Data Protection regulators will be able to impose fines of up to 5% of annual worldwide turnover or €100 million for certain breaches. This is a significant change. In Germany the maximum fine is €300,000 under current legislation, and rarely imposed at all.

2. New data breach notification requirements include broad definitions and short deadlines for the notification of personal data breaches, imposing an imperative on the Data Controller to notify supervisory authorities within 24 hours of discovering a breach.

3. Data subject consent must be explicit to be valid, which would change the current position where consent only needs to be 'explicit' when a business relies on it as a basis for processing sensitive personal data, such as ethnic origin, political opinions or religious beliefs.

PARTICIPATING SECTORS

- 35% Public Sector
- 24% Healthcare
- 21% Financial Services
- 17% Retail
- 3% Transport and Logistics

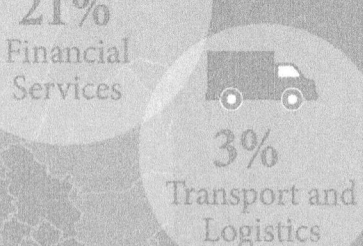

Data Protection

 92%

...of organisations have a designated Data Protection Officer who defines the corporate strategy and requirements for data protection, incorporating both employee and customer information.

 89%

...of organisations have defined Data Processor Agreement and responsibilities with their third parties.

 72%

...of organisations undertake annual Data Protection training to make employees aware of particular Data Protection requirements in their work area.

 72%

...of organisations ensure that all personal data processed by permitted personal devices remains in compliance with the Data Protection Act.

 75%

...of organisations have a defined and practiced Incident Response Plan, involving their key service providers and post-incident customer communications.

 35%

...of organisations have plotted Personal Identifiable Information (PII) touch points with their internal and external parties in a Data permeation Map.

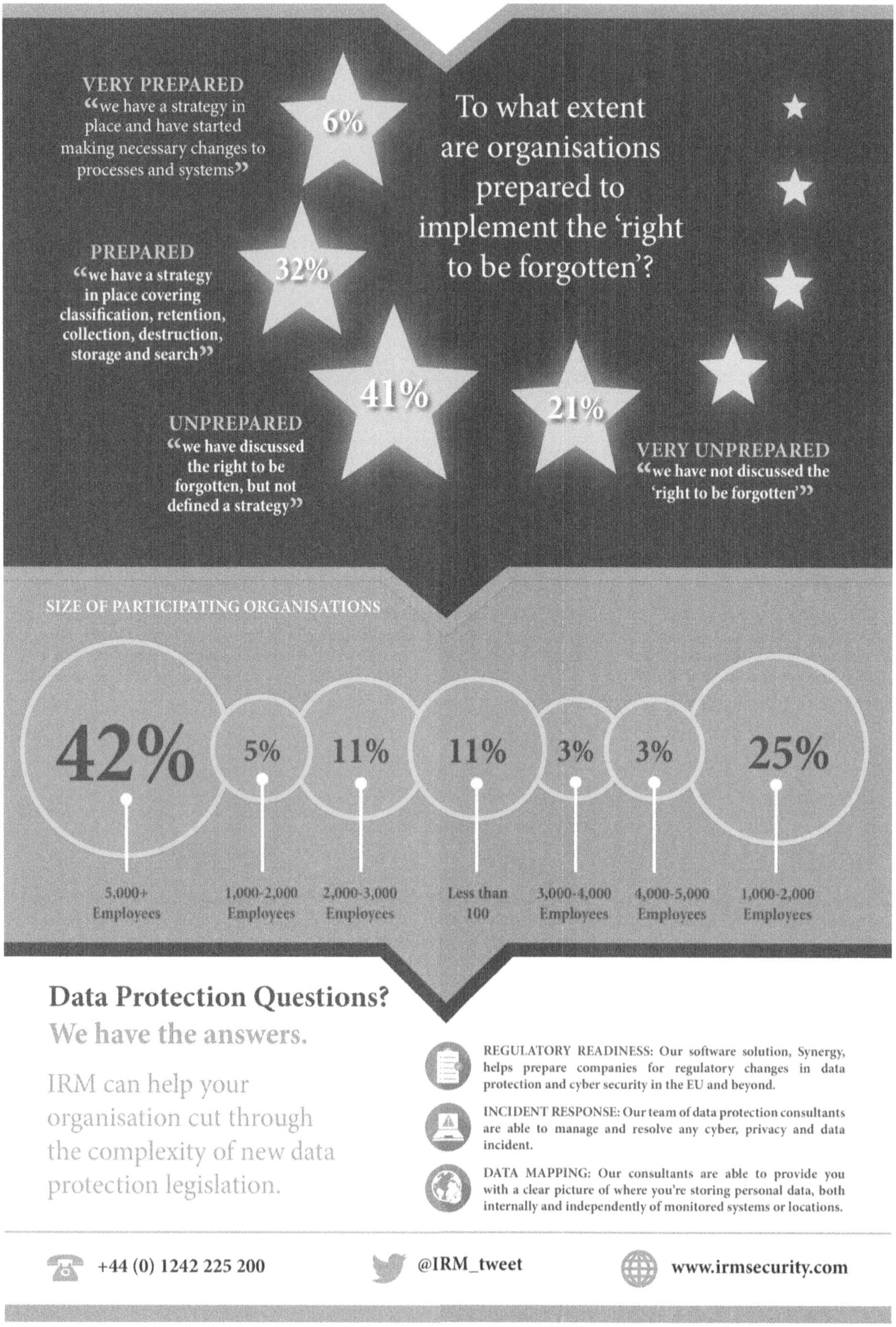

CeMAP 1 Revision Guide

To what extent are organisations prepared to implement the 'right to be forgotten'?

VERY PREPARED — "we have a strategy in place and have started making necessary changes to processes and systems" — **6%**

PREPARED — "we have a strategy in place covering classification, retention, collection, destruction, storage and search" — **32%**

UNPREPARED — "we have discussed the right to be forgotten, but not defined a strategy" — **41%**

VERY UNPREPARED — "we have not discussed the 'right to be forgotten'" — **21%**

SIZE OF PARTICIPATING ORGANISATIONS

%	Employees
42%	5,000+ Employees
5%	1,000-2,000 Employees
11%	2,000-3,000 Employees
11%	Less than 100
3%	3,000-4,000 Employees
3%	4,000-5,000 Employees
25%	1,000-2,000 Employees

Data Protection Questions?
We have the answers.

IRM can help your organisation cut through the complexity of new data protection legislation.

 REGULATORY READINESS: Our software solution, Synergy, helps prepare companies for regulatory changes in data protection and cyber security in the EU and beyond.

 INCIDENT RESPONSE: Our team of data protection consultants are able to manage and resolve any cyber, privacy and data incident.

 DATA MAPPING: Our consultants are able to provide you with a clear picture of where you're storing personal data, both internally and independently of monitored systems or locations.

 +44 (0) 1242 225 200   @IRM_tweet   www.irmsecurity.com

12 Other Legislation

The Pensions Act 2004

- Two major parts to this legislation:
  - Pension Protection Fund;
  - The new Pensions Regulator which replaces OPRA.

The Pension Regulator

- The Pension Regulator has wide powers and will take a proactive and risk-focused approach to regulation.
- Statutory objectives are:
  - To protect the benefits of members of work-based pension schemes;
  - To promote good administration of work-based pension schemes;
  - To reduce the risk of situations arising that may lead to claims for compensation from the Pension Protection Fund.

The Pension Protection Fund

- Protects members of private sector final salary pension schemes whose firms become insolvent.
- Compensates members' schemes in cases of fraud, misappropriation and insolvency.
  - 100% for existing pensioners;
  - 90% for pre-retirement members.

CeMAP 1 Revision Guide

The Pensions Act 2011

- This Act confirms the auto enrolment arrangements for the new NEST provision which begins in 2012

- It puts into law State Pension age changes

- Women's retirement ages will equalise with men's at 65 by 2018

- Gradually increase to 66 by 2020.

- The 2013 Autumn Statement confirmed that the state pension age rise to 68 to be brought forward to the mid-2030s - and the age could rise to 69 by the late 2040s.

"EDITH NEVER WAS VERY GOOD AT PARALLEL PARKING."

Other Legislation

The Lending Code

- This is a voluntary code of practice which sets standards for financial institutions to follow when they are dealing with their personal and small business customers in the United Kingdom.
- It provides valuable protection for customers and explains how firms are expected to deal with them day-to-day and in times of financial difficulties.
- The Lending Code covers subscribers dealings with:
  - Consumers
  - Micro-enterprises (enterprises that employ fewer than 10 persons and have a turnover or annual balance sheet that does not exceed €2 million
  - Charities with an income of less than £1 million
- The Code covers:
  - Current account overdrafts
  - Loans
  - Credit cards
  - Lending to micro-enterprises and charities
- The Code does not apply to non-business borrowing secured on land or to sales finance

"WE'RE LIVING IN A WORLD OF LOWERED EXPECTATIONS."

Banking Conduct of Business Rules

- BCOBS replaced the Banking Code to leave the Lending Code and BCOBS the main focus
- BCOBS contains rules and guidance on:
  - Communications with banking customers and financial promotions;
  - Distance communications, including the requirements of the Distance Marketing Directive and E-commerce Directive;
  - Information to be communicated to banking customers, including appropriate information and statements of account;
  - Post sale requirements on prompt, efficient and fair service, moving accounts and lost and dormant accounts;
  - Unauthorised and incorrectly executed payments; and
  - Cancellation, including the right to cancel and the effects of cancellation.
  - BCOBS applies to accepting deposits to the extent that it does not overlap with the requirements of the Payment Services Regulations (PSRs) relating to payment transactions and payment accounts.
- This means that, broadly:
  - Where a retail banking service is not a payment service within the scope of the PSRs, BCOBS applies in full;
  - Where a retail banking service is a payment service within the scope of the PSRs, parts of BCOBS would not apply.

European Union Directives

- They are issued by the European Union and they are binding upon each member state.
- The objectives have to be met but the choice as to how they are achieved is left to the authorities of each state.
- It's a bit like making a speed limit but leaving it to the local authorities on which speed calming measures to adopt.

Banking

- *Second Banking Directive* gave institutions the freedom to establish credit institutions throughout the European Union.

Investment

- Markets in Financial Instruments Directive
    - MiFID right to operate throughout the EU on the basis of home regulation.
    - Products include shares, unit trusts, futures, forwards and currency dealings.

Life Assurance

- The main objectives of the single market for insurance are to provide all EU citizens with access to the widest possible range of insurance products, whilst ensuring them of the highest standards of legal and financial protection.
- *Second Life Directive* gave freedom to provide life assurance services across Europe.
- *Third Life Directive* gave additional protection to consumers by tightening up the running of insurance companies.
- *Fourth Life Directive* – consolidated all previous directives.

General insurance

- *Second Non-Life Directive* gave freedom to provide general insurance services across Europe.
- *Third Non-Life Directive* stated that an insurance company can establish branches and carry out non-life business, in any other member state under the supervision of the authorities of the member state where the head office is located.

Insurance intermediaries

- The EU wants to ensure that retail markets in insurance are accessible and secure. A Directive was introduced on insurance mediation to establish the freedom for insurance intermediaries to provide services in all states throughout the EU.

13 Specimen Exam

Unit 1 – Introduction to Financial Services Environment and products

1. The Bank of England is a central bank because it:
   a. deposits money with the International Monetary Fund
   b. Has been approved by the Treasury and lends money direct to other banks
   c. Holds reserves of foreign currency for other banks and institutional investors
   d. Acts as banker to the government, supervises the economy and regulates the supply of money

2. Charlie is a US citizen but has been working in the UK for the last 7 months. He may be regarded as UK
   a. Resident
   b. Ordinarily Resident
   c. Domiciled
   d. Deemed Domiciled

3. When a person dies without having made a will and leaves surviving spouse and two children, the surviving spouse has absolute title to:
   a. the first £125,000
   b. the first £250,000
   c. the first £450,000
   d. the entire estate

4. Which one of the following organisations issues permanent interest-bearing shares?
   a. Companies quoted on the London Stock Exchange
   b. Building societies
   c. Local authorities
   d. The Bank of England

5. At what level of annual income does an employee start to be taxed on the value of all benefits in kind?
   a. £2,230
   b. £5,225
   c. £8,200
   d. £8,500

6. What is MOST likely to happen when interest rates rise?
   a. Share prices will rise
   b. With Profit bonus rates will fall
   c. Rates of guaranteed bonds will fall
   d. Annuity rates will rise

7. What is the maximum amount of taxable income which can be chargeable at 20% tax in 2015/2016?
   a. £5,000
   b. £15,240
   c. £27,100
   d. £31,785

8. William is self-employed. He is likely to pay which classes of NI?
   a. Classes 2 and 4
   b. Classes 1 and 3
   c. Classes 3 and 4
   d. Classes 2 and 3

9. An individual dies in December 2015 leaving an estate of £550,000, which £425,000 is left to an old friend, £100,000 to a registered charity, and £25,000 to his political party. What will be the inheritance tax payable?
   a. £40,000
   b. £90,000
   c. £160,000
   d. £210,000

10. If an individual makes a lifetime transfer to a friend, full inheritance tax will arise if, after making the transfer, the individual dies within
    a. 3 years
    b. 5 years
    c. 7 years
    d. 9 years

11. Mr. Trent will potentially incur an inheritance tax liability if he disposes of his valuable Turner painting in which of the following ways?
    a. He gives it to his wife
    b. He sells it to his daughter for a token amount
    c. He sells it at auction when a local dealer would have paid higher price
    d. He leaves it in his will to an historic house owned by the National Trust

12. Alan Smith is a basic rate tax payer and has a total taxable capital gain on the shares he dabbles in of £10,600. His tax in 2015/2016 on the gain will be:
    a. £0
    b. £1,908
    c. £2,120
    d. £2,968

13. Which of the following is liable to income tax but not to capital gains tax?
    a. An art dealer's profit from the sale of a work of art
    b. Antiques sold by an old lady to a dealer for under £6,000
    c. A holiday cottage in Cornwall sold at a profit by a City business person
    d. A win on the horses in a betting shop as opposed to the tote

14. For an employed person, which one of the following would NOT be classed as earned income?
    a. Salary.
    b. Bonuses.
    c. Company share dividends.
    d. Taxable benefits in kind.

15. Mrs. Richards wishes to leave her estate, valued at £600,000, to her three children. How might she minimise the impact of the potential inheritance tax liability?

   a. By gifting £600,000 to her children so that each receives £200,000 on her death
   b. By selling her assets to her children at a token price close to the time that she expects to die
   c. By effecting an own life whole of life policy written under trust with her estate as beneficiary
   d. By effecting an own life whole of life policy written under trust with her children as beneficiaries

16. An employee earns £1,000 per week. His employer will pay National Insurance contributions as a proportion of what part of his earnings?

   a. His total earnings
   b. His earnings between the upper earnings limit and the Primary Threshold only
   c. His earnings up to the upper earnings limit only
   d. His total earnings above the Primary Threshold

17. Entitlement to Jobseekers Allowance in the first six months of claiming is dependent on the individual's:

   a. level of unearned income
   b. amount of savings
   c. National Insurance contributions received
   d. length of time with the employer

18. Which of the following Social Security benefits is means tested

   a. Income support
   b. One parent benefit
   c. Child benefit
   d. Statutory maternity pay

19. An employee who pays Class 1 National Insurance contributions and who is off work for more than four consecutive days because of illness initially receives

   a. Disability living allowance
   b. Carers allowance
   c. Attendance allowance
   d. Statutory sick pay

20. John's level of investment income is such that the higher rate of income tax is payable. He has been claiming Incapacity Benefit for 9 months, what level of income tax will this benefit be subject to?
    a. No tax liability
    b. Tax at the basic rate
    c. Tax at the higher rate
    d. Tax at the difference between basic and higher rate

21. The income benefit paid out under a Permanent Health Insurance policy is treated in which of the following ways for income tax purposes
    a. Completely tax free
    b. Taxed as earned income after the first 12 months' payments
    c. Taxed as unearned income after the first 12 months' payments
    d. Taxed in full from the first payment

22. An individual is likely to pay Class 3 National Insurance Contributions to improve entitlement to
    a. Basic state pension
    b. Severe disablement allowance
    c. Income support
    d. Attendance allowance

23. Social Security benefits
    a. Are only relevant when the client is on a low income
    b. Can be disregarded in financial planning because the benefits are negligible
    c. Must be taken into account when assessing a client's needs, as some needs will be fulfilled by these benefits
    d. Should be taken into account when they are currently being paid to a client

24. Stamp duty land tax is a tax imposed on:
    a. Contracts
    b. Documents
    c. Property
    d. Services

25. Alice earns £60 a week working in a bakery. She has been told this amount is below the Primary Threshold for National Insurance contributions. That means:
   a. She will have to pay 1% contributions
   b. She will have to pay 10.6% and her employer 12% contributions
   c. She will pay nothing and her employer will pay 12.8% contributions
   d. Neither Alice nor her employer need pay contributions

26. In advising self-employed persons on their financial affairs, it should be remembered that
   a. They can expect to receive enhanced sickness benefit from the state
   b. They can expect to receive the maximum benefits available from State Second Pension
   c. They can offset all their National Insurance contributions against their income tax liability
   d. They receive their income without deduction of income tax

27. Which of the following is liable for income tax?
   a. The interest portions of a purchased life annuity
   b. National lottery winnings
   c. Interest on national savings certificates
   d. Income from ISAs

28. Someone claiming the Working Tax Credit would need to:
   a. Be working more than 30 hours per week, unless they're disabled, over 60 or have children.
   b. Already be in receipt of Income Support
   c. Claim it through their employers' payroll
   d. Have a least 2 children

29. Which one of the following would provide a guaranteed income to a client?
   a. Blue chip shares
   b. National Savings Certificates
   c. A with profits bond
   d. A Government Gilt

Specimen Exam

30. Mr and Mrs Grey have a number of financial needs but can't afford to satisfy them all. They ask you to advise them. What should you do?

    a. Ensure their life assurance needs are satisfied and then recommend products to satisfy their other needs to the extent they can afford

    b. Prioritise their needs in consultation with the clients and recommend products to satisfy those needs in order of priority

    c. Ensure adequate protection of income is established before recommending policies to satisfy any other needs

    d. Prioritise their needs against criteria laid down by the FCA and present them with recommendations in order of priority

31. Which one of the following types of investment is most suitable to a client with a lump sum who does not wish to risk losing any capital?

    a. Unit trusts

    b. Unit linked endowment

    c. A REIT

    d. National Savings Income Bond

32. An adviser should suggest that an existing policy be surrendered only if:

    a. It has only recently been taken out

    b. The adviser has a new policy which better suits the client's needs

    c. There are no tax advantages from the existing policy

    d. It is entirely inappropriate for the client's needs

33. What does an open market option allow individuals to do?

    a. Use the tax free cash lump sum to buy a purchased life annuity

    b. Transfer the value of their pension fund to another insurance company prior to selected retirement age

    c. To purchase a deferred annuity at advantageous rates

    d. Use the accumulated pension fund to buy a pensions annuity from any insurance company

2015/2016

34. Miss Rowbottom has a £5,000 business loan which is repayable in one lump sum in ten years' time from business profits. She needs a policy with a sum assured of £5,000 at the lowest cost to provide protection should she die before the loan is repaid. The most suitable policy will be a

   a. Gift Inter Vivos policy
   b. Decreasing term assurance
   c. Level term assurance
   d. Low cost whole life assurance

35. The benefit under a family income benefit policy is

   a. Tax-free
   b. Taxable at basic rate of income tax at source
   c. Paid gross but must be declared for income tax purposes
   d. Paid gross but subject to income tax after 12 months payments

36. Brian requires a life policy to pay out a guaranteed cash value at maturity and needs the level of life cover and premiums to remain fixed throughout the term. Which of the following types of policy would be most suitable?

   a. Non-profit endowment assurance.
   b. Unit-linked endowment assurance.
   c. Universal whole-of-life assurance.
   d. With-profits whole-of-life assurance.

37. Which is NOT a feature of a critical illness policy?

   a. It provides a regular income
   b. It is paid whether or not the assured continues working
   c. It can continue throughout the assured's lifetime
   d. It can cover permanent total disability

38. There are three main elements that make up policy premiums for a term assurance which of the following would be the EXCEPTION?

   a. Claims cost
   b. Investment
   c. Mortality risk
   d. Expenses

39. Which of the following is correct when considering Stakeholder Pensions?
   a. Benefits can be taken from age 45
   b. Non taxpayers can get tax relief on contributions
   c. The annual allowance limit does not apply
   d. Employees in occupational pensions cannot contribute to a stakeholder pension

40. Susan has a part time job and earns just enough to pay income tax. She has decided to contribute to a Stakeholder. How much tax relief will she receive on her contributions?
   a. 10%
   b. 20%
   c. 40%
   d. None

41. Joanne was born on 1st July 1982 and her income is £12,000. What is the maximum contribution she can make into her Stakeholder pension this year?
   a. Nil
   b. £3,600
   c. £12,000
   d. £50,000

42. Mr and Mrs Pope have a joint repayment mortgage with £30,000 outstanding. They have just had their house valued for £90,000. How much equity do they have in their home?
   a. £30,000
   b. £60,000
   c. £90,000
   d. None, the mortgage lender does

43. A capped rate mortgage is
   a. A variable rate mortgage with a minimum rate payable
   b. A mortgage with a fixed rate for the whole of the term
   c. A variable rate mortgage with the option to change to a fixed rate at some point in the future
   d. A variable rate mortgage with a maximum rate payable

44. The contribution period for an ISA is based over the period
   a. 1 April to 31 March.
   b. 6 April to 5 April.
   c. 1 January to 31 December.
   d. 31 January to 31 July.

45. The main purpose for which redundancy protection is offered by insurers is
   a. To provide a lump sum on redundancy
   b. Contribution of pension contributions
   c. Protection of mortgage and loan repayments
   d. Continuation of National Insurance contributions

46. A medium dated gilt has a coupon of 12%. Current interest rates are 7%. Which of the following will cause the market price of the gilt to rise?
   a. A fall in market interest rates
   b. A rise in market interest rates
   c. An increase in the basic rate of income tax
   d. A decrease in the basic rate of income tax

47. Which of the following funds is likely to have the lowest risk?
   a. UK Equity funds
   b. Gilt funds
   c. Managed funds
   d. General and international funds

48. An investment trust is
   a. Another term for a unit trust
   b. Subject to capital gains tax within the fund
   c. Likely to be more risky than a unit trust
   d. Designed with a single pricing structure to be marketed across Europe

49. Which ONE of the following National Savings products could not have a term of five years?
   a. Fixed Interest Certificates
   b. Income Bonds
   c. Guaranteed Growth Bond
   d. Children's Bond

50. What is the main advantage of using a pension plan to support an interest only mortgage?
   a. They often run over a longer term.
   b. They are assigned to the lender.
   c. They guarantee to repay the loan.
   d. They benefit from favourable tax concessions

Unit 2 – UK Financial Services and Regulation

51. Which one of the following is NOT a requirement under the Financial Conduct Authority Core Conduct of Business Rules in respect of dealing for customers?

   a. Sale of shares at the best price available.

   b. Purchase of a term assurance at the lowest rate available.

   c. Dealing at prices which are advantageous for the size and type of transaction.

   d. Justification of switching from the customer's viewpoint.

52. Under the Financial Services Act advising on investments without proper authorisation or exemption is a

   a. Breach of contract

   b. Breach of trust

   c. Criminal offence

   d. Civil offence

53. The Financial Conduct Authority

   a. Regulates the majority of the financial services industry, except banking

   b. Cannot operate until after the Financial Services Act is 3 years old

   c. Is a statutory body

   d. Intends to maintain the existing SIB principles

54. The provisions of the Financial Services Act don't apply to articles in the press

   a. Unless their principle purpose is to persuade readers to invest in a particular investment

   b. If they are only given in response to a readers enquiry

   c. If they have been authorised by the editorial board

   d. If they include recommendations for specific investments provided the newspaper does not hold such investments as a proprietor

55. Who is ultimately responsible for regulating investment business as defined by the Financial Services Act?
   a. The Chief Secretary to the Treasury
   b. The Secretary of State for Trade and Industry
   c. The Chancellor of the Exchequer
   d. The Governor of the Bank of England

56. Under the unsolicited non written financial promotion rules
   a. A salesperson may cold call a prospect at any hour provided that he desists if the prospect does not wish the call
   b. A salesperson may only call during socially acceptable hours and must desist if the prospect does not wish the call to continue
   c. A salesperson can only cold call for investment business the prospect is an existing client and does not object to the call
   d. A salesperson may only call upon a prospect if he has previously sent him a pre-approach letter

57. The FCA's Statement of Principle concerning relations with regulators requires that a firm, in any dealings with the regulator, acts
   a. In an open and co-operative manner
   b. In a timely fashion answering enquiries within 10 days
   c. With reasonable care, skill and diligence
   d. Without prejudice to its client's interests

58. Where an independent financial adviser is giving investment advice to a stockbroker, the stockbroker will be treated as
   a. An execution only customer
   b. A business investor
   c. A professional investor
   d. A market counterparty

59. Full disclosure rules must be complied with each time an adviser recommends
   a. The purchase of a product covered by the rules
   b. The purchase or variation of a product covered by the rules
   c. The purchase or variation of a product covered by the rules, but only where that variation involves an increase in premium
   d. Any advice on a non-packaged investment product

60. Under what circumstances should a restricted adviser recommend a client to an independent adviser?
    a. If another company offers the same product with a lower premium.
    b. If the client insists on best advice.
    c. If the company they represent has no suitable product.
    d. Under no circumstances

61. The "know your client" rule requires
    a. A face to face interview with a client
    b. Completion of a limited financial questionnaire
    c. The advisor should obtain proper knowledge of a customer's financial circumstances and needs
    d. Completion of a detailed factfind for the advisor's records

62. Which rule comes into effect when it could be inferred that an independent intermediary has a vested interest in a product being sold?
    a. Best advice.
    b. Reason why.
    c. Better than best advice.
    d. Know your customer.

63. Who would be most likely to be affected by the 'best execution' rule?
    a. Stockbrokers.
    b. Independent intermediaries.
    c. Company representatives.
    d. Tied agents

64. The frequency of compliance visits by the FCA's officers to a particular firm depends on the:
    a. A number of approved individuals employed by the firm.
    b. size of the firm, measured by its gross income.
    c. type of firm.
    d. regulator's risk assessment of the firm.

65. As a restricted adviser, you find that your clients need a product that your company cannot provide. To ensure that our clients are best served you

    a. Refer them to a tied agent of a company who have the right product
    b. Offer the best alternative product you have in your product range
    c. Refer them to an independent adviser
    d. Refer them to a tied representative providing you have a formal referral agreement

66. James works as an IFA for Hedge Advisers, and is managed by Julie. Hedge is a member of Hybrid, an IFA network. Who has to accept ultimate responsibility for James's authorisation?

    a. James
    b. Julie
    c. Hybrid
    d. Hedge Advisers

67. In which document will a retail client find a written explanation of advice and the possible benefits and disadvantages of entering into a transaction?

    a. A cancellation notice.
    b. A client agreement.
    c. A key features document.
    d. A suitability report.

68. When advising customers, a restricted single tied adviser must

    a. only provide advice on products from a panel of providers.
    b. only provide advice on the products of the provider she represents.
    c. provide advice on all products, but can only sell the products of the company she represents.
    d. provide advice on and sell all products from the marketplace.

69. Under the Financial Services Act Cancellation Rules, if a cancellation notice is completed and returned within 14 days the client of; regular premium unit linked life policy is entitled to;

    a. The bid value of units
    b. The offer price, less any shortfall between the investment and cancellation dates
    c. A full refund of premiums
    d. Nothing

70. An execution-only sale is one where
    a. The adviser has to deal in investment at a price that is no worse than the best available for the size of deal
    b. The client requests advice in a specific investment are and instructs the adviser to select the best product in that area
    c. The adviser recommends the best policy available, but the client requests that no information on this circumstances is documented
    d. The client requests a specific product and no advice is requested or received

71. A large firm of advisers is required to have all of the following EXCEPT?
    a. Complaints officer
    b. Training & Competence Scheme Officer
    c. Compliance officer
    d. Money Laundering Reporting Officer

72. Which of the following is NOT correct in respect of client money
    a. Is must be held in a separate bank account
    b. It must be held at an approved bank
    c. It must be held on trust for the client
    d. It must be in the name of the firm but include "trust account" in the title

73. "Better than best advice" must be given when
    a. A multi tied agent recommends a product of one company over another
    b. Independent intermediaries recommend a product with which they are a 'connected person'
    c. A tied agent introduces a client to an independent financial advisor
    d. An independent intermediary recommends an insurer which has good investment performance but poor administration

74. The requirement that an investment adviser should not unreasonably churn a customer's investment or unnecessarily switch a customer's policies is
    a. One of the FCA's statements of principle
    b. One of the FCA's conduct of business rules
    c. An ethical principle with no standing in law
    d. A professional code of practice

75. Which one of the following criteria is not one that must be satisfied by an advertisement in order to comply with the Financial Conduct Authority's guidelines on advertising?

    a. It must be fair and not misleading.
    b. It must be authorised by the Financial Conduct Authority.
    c. It must be tailored to the likely level of sophistication of the reader.
    d. It must clearly state the tax position in respect of contributions and benefits.

76. An appointed representative gives bad financial advice to a customer as a result of which she suffers loss. To complain, she should approach in the first instance

    a. The company to whom the appointed representative is tied
    b. The Financial Services Compensation Scheme
    c. The Treasury
    d. The FCA

77. The Financial Services Compensation Scheme is available to investors who

    a. Have suffered financial loss through adverse movement in market prices
    b. Have suffered loss from an authorised firm which has ceased business or is likely to do so
    c. Have suffered loss due to receiving bad advice from an unauthorised firm
    d. Have received bad advice from an authorised adviser who has no professional indemnity insurance

78. Marcus is a financial adviser with an IFA firm. Why is he NOT required to undertake a programme of Continuing Professional Development (CPD)?

    a. The firm has nine or less designated individuals.
    b. The firm is the IFA arm of a building society.
    c. He has yet to attain competent status.
    d. He only advises on corporate products.

79. Which of the following complaint related statements is NOT true?
   a. Copies should be kept on file of all investment complaint correspondence.
   b. Telephone complaints are more serious than written complaints.
   c. Complaints must be acknowledged immediately, dealt with promptly and recorded.
   d. The complaints record is examined as part of compliance visits.

80. How are the costs of the Financial Services Compensation Scheme funded?
   a. A levy on authorised firms.
   b. By contingency insurance arrangements.
   c. By direct funding from the Treasury.
   d. By levying a fixed charge on every policy issued.

81. A client has invested £50,000 in the Insecure Bank Ltd which is now become unable to meet its liabilities. What is the maximum he would receive from the deposit fund of the Financial Services Compensation Scheme?
   a. £31,700
   b. £33,000
   c. £50,000
   d. £85,000

82. Which of the following could NOT be used to demonstrate an appropriate level of an adviser's generic knowledge?
   a. The CeFA qualification
   b. The CF qualification
   c. A CPD log
   d. The Institute of Chartered Accountants qualifications

83. Under the Money Laundering regulations, it is an offence to:
   a. Accept any investment business without proof of identity.
   b. Make a malicious report on a suspect.
   c. Tip off a suspect that an investigation is being held.
   d. Appoint a money laundering officer with a criminal record.

84. Under the Money Laundering regulations, where a member of staff suspects a client of money laundering he/she
    a. Must immediately suspend activities on the client's account.
    b. Cannot take any action until firm evidence is received.
    c. Is obliged to investigate the matter further.
    d. Has a legal obligation to report the details.

85. The money laundering regulations require all life offices to put in place a money laundering
    a. Telephone helpline.
    b. Training programme.
    c. Indemnity scheme.
    d. Investigations department.

86. In pointing out the merits of an investment he is recommending, a salesperson must
    a. Explain every detail of the product he recommends
    b. Merely highlight the benefits of his proposal and how they meet his client's needs
    c. Show how the benefits meet the client's needs but also make sure the client understands the product
    d. Gloss over the less attractive elements of the product to his client

87. Jane is arranging a loan secured on her residential property, post-October 2004, but which is not subject to Financial Conduct Authority regulation. This is because:
    a. The security for the loan is a second charge.
    b. The loan is for a purpose other than house purchase.
    c. The loan is for less than £25,000.
    d. The term of the loan is less than ten years.

88. To whom must the compliance manual be available for inspection?
    a. All employees.
    b. All employed representatives only.
    c. All employed and self-employed representatives only.
    d. All employees and representatives.

89. If you work for an insurance company and give bad financial advice to Mrs Telford, as a result of which she suffers loss, she should approach in the first instance the:
   a. Company that employs you.
   b. Investors Compensation Scheme.
   c. Insurance Ombudsman.
   d. Trading Standards Office.

90. Under the Proceeds of Crime Act 2002, where money laundering is suspected, disclosure must be made either to the firm's Money Laundering Reporting Officer or to the
   a. Department for Business Innovation & Skills.
   b. Joint Money Laundering Steering Group.
   c. National Crime Agency.
   d. Treasury Select Committee

91. Mortgage 4 U Ltd has found that their primary method of obtaining new business is NOT permitted under Financial Conduct Authority regulation. This means that they must have been using which of the following methods?
   a. TV Advertising.
   b. Cold calling.
   c. Mortgage Introducers.
   d. Radio Advertising.

92. Sam has received a personalised key facts illustration containing more elements than usual relating to the specific nature of the product and its additional risks. What type of mortgage product must she be arranging?
   a. A lifetime mortgage.
   b. A cash-back mortgage
   c. A re-mortgage.
   d. A further advance.

93. Bob works in the back office of a general insurance broker. From January 2005 he was required to be authorised through the same processes of permission and approval as apply to the remainder of the industry. This is because he:
   a. Has less than 12 months experience in the general insurance industry.
   b. Works on processing insurance claims on behalf of clients.
   c. Is a qualified mortgage adviser.
   d. Arranges for general advertising and marketing of the brokers' services.

94. The Financial Ombudsman Service
    a. Has replaced the Pensions Ombudsman
    b. Has replaced the Insurance Ombudsman
    c. Can make awards binding on authorised firms without limits
    d. Can make awards binding on the complainant

95. On what basis must an IFA report, to their regulator, detail all sums of money received from clients?
    a. Daily
    b. Monthly
    c. Annually
    d. Every 5 years

96. In relation to the Data Protection Act 1998, which one of the following is INCORRECT?
    a. It requires anyone holding computerised data on individuals to be registered.
    b. It gives individuals the right of access to data relating to them.
    c. It applies only to records held on computer.
    d. It requires anyone holding data to have a data protection policy.

97. In addition to the names and addresses of all data controllers who have registered, what other information is included in the Register of Data Controllers?
    a. Broad details of the data they process in terms of type, purpose and the people to whom they want to give information.
    b. Specific details of the data they process in terms of names, National Insurance numbers and dates of birth.
    c. Broad details of the data they process on individuals' credit rating and other personal details.
    d. Specific details of data they process on individuals' tax liabilities and bank deposit accounts held.

98. Which ONE of the following contracts would be subject to the provisions of the Unfair Terms in Consumer Contracts Regulations 1999?
   a. A contract between two businesses for the supply of gas piping.
   b. A contract for the sale of a house between a private seller and private buyer.
   c. An individually negotiated contract for the sale of a fitted kitchen.
   d. A standard service contract between an electrical company and a consumer.

99. Kevin has approached Colin to discuss pensions following a referral from Kevin's client Darren. Colin asks who suggested that he might be interested in pensions. What should Kevin do?
   a. Decline to answer as he has been requested not to divulge Darren's name
   b. Give Darren's name having obtained his permission at the outset to do so.
   c. Give Darren's name and explain briefly the nature of Darren's business with the company.
   d. State that he must first obtain the clients permission to reveal his name.

100. What is 'better than best' advice?
   a. Advice which shows a product to be better than any other.
   b. Advice for which an adviser shares his remuneration,
   c. A recommendation by a tied agent that a client should consult an IFA.
   d. Extra careful advice arising from a conflict of interest.

Although they restricted themselves to one drink at lunch time, Howard and Tom still found they were not at their most productive in the afternoons

Answers

1. D	41. C	81. C
2. A	42. B	82. C
3. B	43. D	83. C
4. B	44. B	84. D
5. D	45. C	85. B
6. D	46. A	86. C
7. D	47. B	87. A
8. A	48. C	88. D
9. A	49. B	89. A
10. A	50. D	90. C
11. B	51. B	91. B
12. A	52. C	92. A
13. A	53. C	93. D
14. C	54. A	94. B
15. D	55. C	95. C
16. D	56. B	96. C
17. C	57. A	97. A
18. A	58. D	98. D
19. D	59. B	99. B
20. C	60. C	100. D
21. A	61. C	
22. A	62. C	
23. C	63. A	
24. C	64. D	
25. D	65. C	
26. D	66. C	
27. A	67. D	
28. A	68. B	
29. D	69. C	
30. B	70. D	
31. D	71. A	
32. D	72. D	
33. D	73. B	
34. C	74. B	
35. A	75. B	
36. A	76. A	
37. A	77. B	
38. B	78. C	
39. B	79. B	
40. B	80. A	

Lightning Source UK Ltd.
Milton Keynes UK
UKOW07f1426211015

261079UK00003B/13/P